SAUCE BASICS

MY COOKING CLASS

SAUCE BASICS

87 RECIPES
ILLUSTRATED STEP BY STEP

KEDA BLACK
PHOTOGRAPHS BY FRÉDÉRIC LUCANO

FIREFLY BOOKS

Published by Firefly Books Ltd. 2010

First printing

Publisher Cataloging-in-Publication Data (U.S.)
Black, Keda.
Sauce basics : 87 recipes illustrated step by step / Keda Black ; photographs by Frédéric Lucano.
[256] p. : col. photos. ; cm.
Includes index.
ISBN-13: 978-1-55407-761-8 (pbk.)
ISBN-10: 1-55407-761-3 (pbk.)
1. Sauces. I. Lucano, Frédéric. II. Title.
641.814 dc22 TX819.A1.B53 2010

Library and Archives Canada Cataloguing in Publication
Black, Keda
Sauce basics : 87 recipes illustrated step by step / Keda Black.
Includes index.
ISBN-13: 978-1-55407-761-8 (pbk.)
ISBN-10: 1-55407-761-3 (pbk.)
1. Sauces. I. Title.
TX819.A1B54 2010 641.8'14 C2010-901574-6

Published in the United States by
Firefly Books (U.S.) Inc.
P.O. Box 1338, Ellicott Station
Buffalo, New York 14205

Published in Canada by
Firefly Books Ltd.
66 Leek Crescent
Richmond Hill, Ontario L4B 1H1

Printed in China

PREFACE

Sauces: overused, disliked, forgotten, manufactured, ruined . . . This book will allow you to regain control. Arm yourself with a whisk and a good knife, and master once and for all the essential accessory to simple yet tasty food. The proof is illustrated step-by-step. Before your eyes, béarnaise will become a no-fail sauce and mayonnaise will become easy and attainable. You'll learn how to liven up, in 10 minutes and with three cuts of a knife, the dullest of leftover roasts or serve steamed vegetables, grilled meats or a simple ice cream without ever being monotonous.

Meat, fish, pasta, vegetables or desserts, cold or roasted, raw or boiled . . . Whatever the dish or style of cooking, you will find one or several sauces that perfectly match your meal. We get started with an anthology of the great classics (marchand de vin, aioli, blue cheese), which is followed by a series of Italian temptations (pestos and tomato sauces). Next, a collection of salsas, chutneys and other fresh ideas will surprise you with their lightness and powerful flavors, and then vinaigrettes will make you forget all your worries. Lastly, you'll discover a few knockout foams and, as a bonus, pure delight in the form of dessert sauces (lemon, caramel, whipped cream, crème anglaise).

Interspersed within the recipes are ideas that showcase the sauces, of which you're sure to be very proud. And that is only the beginning: follow our instructions and learn how to marry foods (lamb chops with roasted zucchini coulis, shrimp with vanilla sauce), but don't hesitate to dream up your own variations and combinations.

It's your turn to play!

✻ ✻ ✻

CONTENTS

THE CLASSICS

1

THE ESSENTIALS

THE MAYONNAISES

RECIPE IDEAS

Some sauces are accompanied by a recipe idea, which is indicated with the recipe number and an asterisk symbol (*).

1

BÉCHAMEL

YIELD: 2½ CUPS (625 ML) • PREPARATION: 15 MINUTES • COOKING: 30 MINUTES

½ onion
2 cloves
2½ cups (625 ml) milk

1 bay leaf
3 tablespoons (45 ml) butter
⅓ cup (75 ml) flour

Salt & pepper, to taste
1 pinch freshly grated nutmeg

1	Prick the onion with the cloves. Simmer the milk, the onion with cloves and the bay leaf over low heat for 15 minutes. Once the milk is flavored, remove the seasonings and discard.	2	In a saucepan, gently melt the butter over medium heat.
3	Remove the butter from the heat, add the flour and mix with a wooden spoon.	4	Cook the butter-flour mixture over low heat for 2 to 3 minutes.

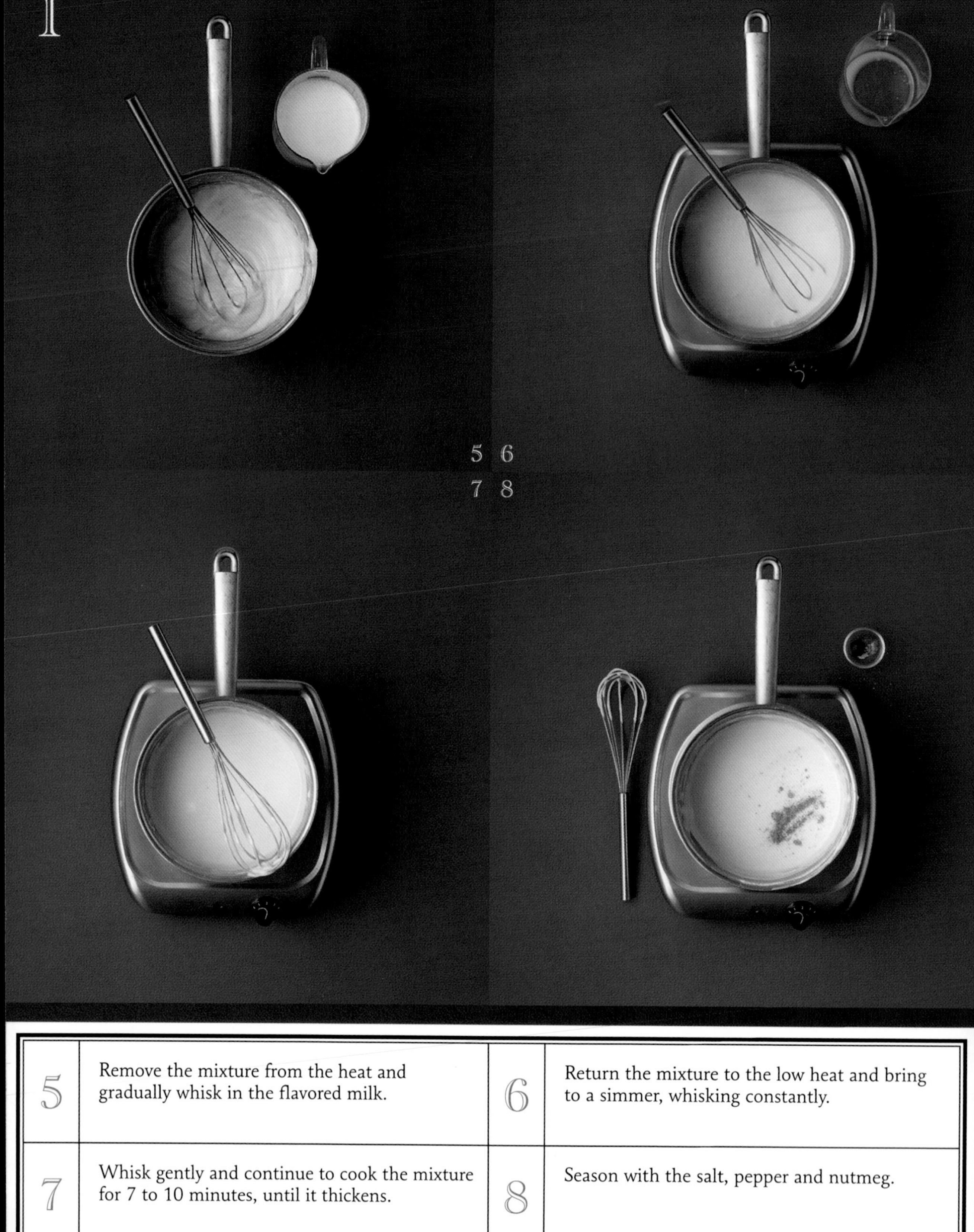

5	Remove the mixture from the heat and gradually whisk in the flavored milk.	6	Return the mixture to the low heat and bring to a simmer, whisking constantly.
7	Whisk gently and continue to cook the mixture for 7 to 10 minutes, until it thickens.	8	Season with the salt, pepper and nutmeg.

9 The sauce is ready. You can use béchamel in a lasagna (see recipe idea 1*).

STORAGE

Place plastic wrap directly on top of the sauce to prevent a skin from forming on its surface.

VARIATION

You can reduce the amounts of butter and flour by half to make a lighter sauce, or you can increase them by half to make a thicker sauce (as a base for a soufflé or to thicken the sauce of a simmered dish).

2

BÉARNAISE

✦ **YIELD: ABOUT ½ CUP (125 ML)** • PREPARATION: 15 MINUTES • COOKING: 20 MINUTES ✦

1 shallot
⅔ cup (150 ml) butter
¼ cup (60 ml) tarragon vinegar or white wine vinegar

4 black peppercorns, crushed
3 sprigs tarragon
2 egg yolks
Salt, to taste

PRELIMINARY:
Peel and finely chop the shallot.

1 2

3 4

1	Clarify the butter by melting it over very low heat and allowing it to bubble for 10 to 15 minutes.	2	Filter the butter through a strainer lined with cheesecloth to remove the white foam.	
3	Place the chopped shallot in a small saucepan along with the vinegar, pepper and tarragon.	4	Bring to a boil and reduce to about two-thirds.	➢

5	Place the egg yolks in a double-boiler over low heat.	6	Filter the reduced vinegar through a fine strainer and discard the pepper and tarragon. Whisk the strained vinegar into the egg yolks.
7	Gradually whisk the clarified butter into the vinegar mixture. Once half the butter has been mixed in, turn off the heat.	8	Take the saucepan off the heat and finish whisking in the butter, until the sauce is creamy and thick.

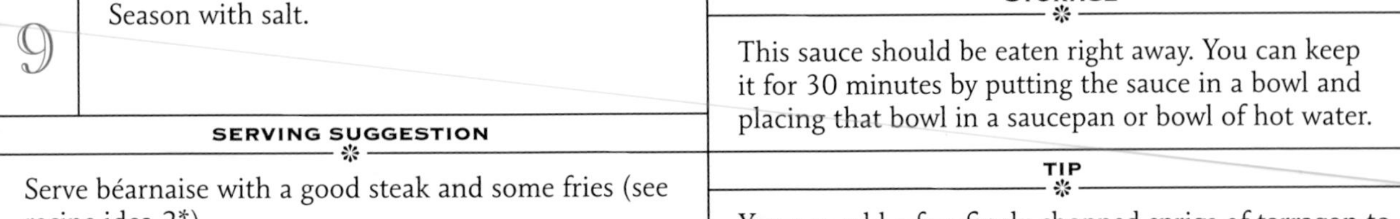

9 Season with salt.

SERVING SUGGESTION

Serve béarnaise with a good steak and some fries (see recipe idea 2*).

STORAGE

This sauce should be eaten right away. You can keep it for 30 minutes by putting the sauce in a bowl and placing that bowl in a saucepan or bowl of hot water.

TIP

You can add a few finely chopped sprigs of tarragon to the final sauce.

LASAGNA

YIELD: 2 SERVINGS • INCLUDES ½ BATCH OF BÉCHAMEL

1. Cook 2 salmon fillets. Season the fish with salt, pepper and a little lemon juice, and flake it.
2. In a covered saucepan, cook 1 pound (500 g) spinach with 1 tablespoon (15 ml) butter and a little salt, pepper and finely chopped fresh chili pepper for 10 minutes over low heat.
3. In a buttered baking dish, alternate layers of lasagna noodles, flaked salmon and spinach. Finish with a layer of lasagna noodles and cover with béchamel sauce.
4. Bake in a 350°F (180°C) oven for 20 minutes.

STEAK & FRIES WITH BÉARNAISE

YIELD: 2 SERVINGS • INCLUDES 1 BATCH OF BÉARNAISE

✣ 1. Prepare the béarnaise and set it aside in a bowl in hot water.
✣ 2. Sear 2 oiled and peppered steaks in a hot skillet or grill pan.
✣ 3. Prepare the fries.
✣ 4. Season the steaks with salt then serve with the sauce and fries.

CLASSIC HOLLANDAISE

YIELD: ABOUT ⅔ CUP (150 ML) • PREPARATION: 5 MINUTES • COOKING: 15 MINUTES

½ cup (125 ml) butter
3 egg yolks
1 tablespoon (15 ml) lemon juice
Salt & pepper, to taste

CLARIFYING THE BUTTER:
Melt the butter over low heat, let bubble for 10 to 15 minutes and then filter through a strainer lined with cheesecloth.

SERVING SUGGESTIONS:
Serve with cooked vegetables (such as asparagus, artichokes and new potatoes).

1 2

3 4

1	Place the egg yolks and lemon juice in a blender.	2	Blend until the mixture is foamy.
3	Gradually add the clarified butter in a thin stream while blending.	4	Season with salt and pepper and It's ready! The sauce should be served immediately (it can, however, be set aside for 30 minutes in a bowl in hot water).

ORANGE HOLLANDAISE

VARIATION OF CLASSIC HOLLANDAISE

⁘ 1. Follow the method outlined in recipe 3, but substitute orange juice for the lemon juice.

⁘ 2. You can sprinkle a little grated orange zest over the sauce at the end.

SERVING SUGGESTION: Boiled vegetables, such as baby artichokes (see recipe idea 4*).

EGG-WHITE HOLLANDAISE

VARIATION OF CLASSIC HOLLANDAISE

✣ 1. Prepare the hollandaise sauce (see recipe 3).
✣ 2. Whisk 3 egg whites until stiff.
✣ 3. Using a skimmer, carefully fold the egg whites into the prepared hollandaise.

It's ready! The egg whites make the sauce lighter, and it can also be stored overnight in the refrigerator.

SERVING SUGGESTIONS: Asparagus or new potatoes.

BEURRE BLANC

YIELD: ABOUT 1 CUP (250 ML) • PREPARATION: 15 MINUTES • COOKING: 10 MINUTES

1 shallot
½ cup (125 ml) cold butter
7 tablespoons (105 ml) dry white wine, e.g., Muscadet (about a small glass)
3 tablespoons (45 ml) white wine vinegar
Salt & pepper, to taste

PRELIMINARY:
Finely chop the shallot and cut the butter into little pieces.

1 2

3 4

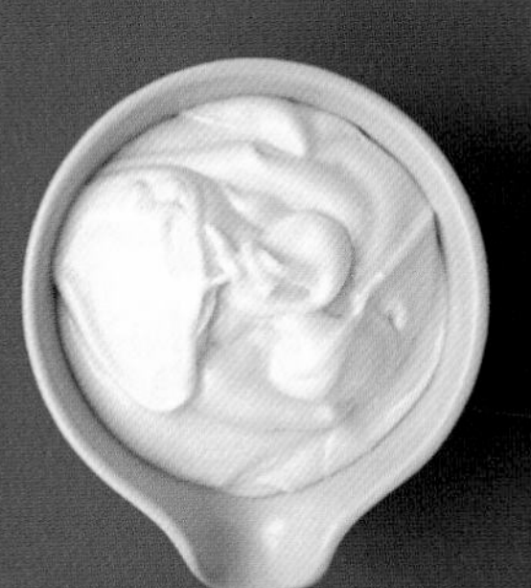

1	Heat the wine, vinegar and shallot in a small saucepan over low heat. Season with salt and pepper.	2	Reduce the wine-vinegar mixture to three-quarters and take the saucepan off the heat. Strain the reduction, return it to the saucepan and discard the shallot.
3	Gradually whisk in the butter. You can return the saucepan to a very low heat if necessary to incorporate the butter, but the butter should never melt, only soften.	4	Check the seasoning, adjust as needed and then serve immediately. See recipe idea 6* for a serving suggestion.

4*

BABY ARTICHOKES WITH ORANGE HOLLANDAISE

YIELD: 4 SERVINGS • INCLUDES 1 BATCH OF ORANGE HOLLANDAISE

❖ 1. Prepare 1 bunch baby artichokes by removing the stems and any hard leaves.

❖ 2. Boil in salted water for 5 to 7 minutes.

❖ 3. Serve with the sauce and a little orange zest. Artichokes also go well with green sauce with orange (see recipe 47).

SOLE WITH BEURRE BLANC

YIELD: 4 SERVINGS • INCLUDES 1 BATCH OF BEURRE BLANC

- 1. Peel and cook some new potatoes.
- 2. Grill, fry or steam 8 sole fillets.
- 3. Serve the sole with the beurre blanc and new potatoes.

7

BLUE CHEESE SAUCE

YIELD: ABOUT 1 CUP (250 ML) • PREPARATION: 5 MINUTES • COOKING: 5 MINUTES

3½ ounces (100 g) blue cheese
⅔ cup (150 ml) crème fraîche or sour cream
¼ cup (60 ml) Greek-style yogurt (optional)
Ground pepper, to taste

NOTE:
You can combine several types of blue cheese, such as Roquefort, Gorgonzola, Bresse bleu.

SERVING SUGGESTION:
Grilled meat and potatoes (see recipe idea 7*).

1 2

3 4

1	Put the cheese and crème fraîche in a small saucepan.	2	Gently melt the cheese and bring the mixture to a boil, stirring constantly.
3	Take the saucepan off the heat as soon as the sauce adheres to a wooden spoon. Add the yogurt for a lighter sauce with a touch of acidity.	4	Season with salt, if needed (season with care, as the cheese is already salty), and pepper.

8

GREEN PEPPERCORN SAUCE

YIELD: ABOUT 1 CUP (250 ML) • PREPARATION: 10 MINUTES • COOKING: 15 MINUTES

1 shallot
½ cup (125 ml) white wine vinegar
2 to 3 teaspoons (10 to 15 ml) canned or jarred green peppercorns

1 cup (250 ml) crème fraîche or sour cream
2 teaspoons (10 ml) Dijon mustard

PRELIMINARY:
Finely slice the shallot.

1	Gently bring the vinegar and 1 small glass of water to a boil.	2	Add the shallot. Reduce until you obtain 2 tablespoons (30 ml) of liquid.	3	Strain the vinegar reduction and discard the shallot. Add the peppercorns to the reduction.
4	Return the reduction to the heat and add the crème fraîche and mustard. Gently bring to a boil.	5	Reduce over very low heat for 2 to 3 minutes.	6	It's ready! Check the seasoning, adjust as needed and serve with beef (see recipe idea 8*).

7*

STEAK WITH BLUE CHEESE SAUCE

YIELD: 2 SERVINGS • INCLUDES 1 BATCH OF BLUE CHEESE SAUCE

✧ 1. Cook 2 oiled beefsteaks in a skillet or grill pan.
✧ 2. Coarsely chop a couple of potatoes and lightly brown.

✧ 3. Serve the steaks with the blue cheese sauce and a little chopped chervil, if desired. Accompany with the fried potatoes.

CHOPPED STEAK WITH GREEN PEPPERCORNS

YIELD: 2 SERVINGS • INCLUDES 1 BATCH OF GREEN PEPPERCORN SAUCE

✧ 1. Cook 2 chopped steaks in a little olive oil.

✧ 2. Top the steaks with the sauce and serve with homemade mashed potatoes and green beans.

MASHED POTATOES: Boil 4 potatoes that you've washed but not peeled. Remove the skin and mash with 1½ tablespoons (22 ml) butter and about ½ to ¾ cup warm milk. Season with salt and pepper.

BERCY SAUCE

YIELD: 2½ CUPS (625 ML) • PREPARATION: 15 MINUTES • COOKING: 45 MINUTES

2½ cups (625 ml) chicken or vegetable stock (preferably homemade or organic)
¼ cup (60 ml) butter
⅓ cup (75 ml) flour

Salt & pepper, to taste
1 shallot
1 cup (250 ml) dry white wine

PRELIMINARY:
Heat the stock. (If using a packaged bouillon, dissolve in boiling water, and if using concentrated broth, dilute in boiling water.

1 2

3 4

1	Melt two-thirds of the butter (about 2½ tablespoons/40 ml) in a saucepan. Add the flour and stir.	2	Cook the roux over low heat, stirring constantly, for 5 to 6 minutes, until lightly browned.	
3	Let cool for a few minutes, and then gradually whisk in the heated stock.	4	Place back over low heat and bring to a simmer, whisking. Cook gently for 20 minutes, until the sauce adheres to the spoon. Season with salt and pepper.	➢

5 6

7 8

5	Chop the shallot very finely.	6	Fry the chopped shallot in the remaining butter, but do not brown.
7	Add the white wine to the shallot and cook until reduced by half.	8	Add the white whine reduction to the stock mixture.

9	Mix well, until the sauce is uniform.	**SERVING SUGGESTION** This sauce can be served with poultry or vegetables (see recipe idea 9*).

NOTE

This sauce is from the velouté family and is the cousin of béchamel (Bercy sauce is béchamel made with stock instead of milk).

VARIATION

You can substitute fish stock for the poultry or vegetable stock to accompany fish.

MARCHAND DE VIN SAUCE

YIELD: ABOUT 3 CUPS (750 ML) • PREPARATION: 25 MINUTES • COOKING: 55 MINUTES

1 small red onion
3½ ounces (100 g) white mushrooms
3 tablespoons (45 ml) butter
1 tablespoon (15 ml) sugar
½ cup (125 ml) red wine
2½ cups (625 ml) beef or vegetable stock (preferably homemade or organic)
1 to 2 sprigs thyme
2½ tablespoons (37 ml) flour
Salt and pepper, to taste

1 2

3 4

1	Chop the onion and mushrooms.	2	Brown the onion in ½ tablespoon (7 ml) butter for 3 to 4 minutes over fairly high heat.	
3	Add the sugar and stir until the sugar starts to caramelize.	4	Remove from the heat and whisk in ¼ cup (60 ml) of the wine. Return to the heat and boil for 2 to 3 minutes.	➢

5	Add 2 cups (½ L) of the stock and the thyme and boil for 4 minutes.	6	Strain the mixture. Set the liquid aside and discard the onions.
7	Melt 1 tablespoon (15 ml) butter, add the flour and cook over low heat, stirring for 5 to 8 minutes, until the mixture browns.	8	Whisk in the strained mixture and bring to a boil.

9	Cook for 5 minutes, stirring until the sauce thickens.	**OPTION** You don't have to use mushrooms and, if you prefer, can stop at this step. In this case, use all the wine in step four and all the stock in step five.

10	Cook the mushrooms in the remaining butter.	11	Add the remaining stock and wine, and simmer for 10 minutes.
12	Add the mushrooms to the sauce.	13	Reduce for another 10 minutes over low heat.

14	Season with salt and pepper.	**TIP**
		Wines from the Corbières region of France work well in this sauce.

SERVING SUGGESTION	**VARIATION**
This sauce goes well with meat as well as eggs (see recipe idea 10*).	For a more acidic sauce, add a little lemon or sherry wine vinegar at the same time as the wine.

FISH PIE

YIELD: 4 SERVINGS • INCLUDES 1 BATCH OF BERCY SAUCE

✧ 1. Slice a few carrots into rounds. Clean ½ head broccoli and separate the florets from the stem.
✧ 2. Steam the vegetables. Cook some fish in a court bouillon or steam it.
✧ 3. Mix the vegetables, fish and Bercy sauce.
✧ 4. Divide a batch of shortcrust pastry in two. Line a baking dish (bottom and sides) with half of the pastry. Add the filling and cover with the other half of the pastry. Bake in a 350°F (180°C) oven for 30 minutes.

STEAK WITH MARCHAND DE VIN SAUC

YIELD: 2 SERVINGS • INCLUDES ½ BATCH OF MARCHAND DE VIN SAUCE

❖ 1. Cook 2 oiled and peppered steaks in a skillet.
❖ 2. Serve with marchand de vin sauce, sautéed potatoes and spinach.

SAUTÉED POTATOES:
Clean the potatoes, cut into chunks and brown over medium heat in a skillet with a little oil, turning them so they cook evenly.

11

MEAT GRAVY

YIELD: ABOUT 3/4 CUP (175 ML) • PREPARATION: 5 MINUTES • COOKING: 10 MINUTES

Drippings from meat (such as cutlets) cooked in a skillet
½ cup (125 ml) wine (red or white, depending on the meat)
2 sprigs flat-leaf parsley

PRELIMINARY:
Wash and drain the parsley. Pluck the leaves from the stems, discard the stems and chop the leaves.

TIP: You can add 2 tablespoons (30 ml) sour cream halfway through the cooking process or a knob of butter at the end to make a richer gravy. For a thicker gravy, add 1 tablespoon (15 ml) flour and cook for 2 to 3 minutes before adding the wine.

1	Remove as much fat as possible from the meat drippings. Reheat the drippings if they are cold.	2	Over medium-high heat, add the wine, scrape the bits of meat stuck to the bottom of the skillet and then bring the mixture to a boil.
3	Let reduce for a few minutes. Strain the gravy.	4	Add the parsley. Gravy can be prepared right after the meat has finished cooking or with drippings from meat prepared the day before. Store drippings in the refrigerator. Serve gravy with meat or a good sausage (see recipe idea 11*).

GRIBICHE SAUCE

→ YIELD: 4 TO 6 SERVINGS • PREPARATION: 20 MINUTES • COOKING: 9 MINUTES ←

3 eggs
1 tablespoon (15 ml) mustard
1 teaspoon (5 ml) red wine vinegar
Salt & ground pepper, to taste

6 sprigs flat-leaf parsley
6 chives
6 sprigs chervil
1 sprig tarragon

¾ ounce (25 g) cornichons or gherkins (about 2 or 3)
1½ tablespoons (22 ml) capers
1½ cups (375 ml) oil

1	Boil the eggs for 9 minutes from the time the water begins to boil; the eggs should be hard-boiled.	2	Peel the eggs' shells.	
3	Using a fork, mash the egg yolks through a strainer and into a large bowl.	4	Add the mustard, vinegar, salt and pepper.	➢

5 6
7 8

5	Wash and dry the herbs. Pluck the leaves from the stems, discard the stems and finely chop the leaves. Finely chop the egg whites, pickles and capers.	6	Pouring in a thin stream, gradually whisk the oil into the egg yolk mixture, as you would to make mayonnaise.
7	Next add the finely chopped herbs, pickles and capers.	8	Finish by adding the egg whites.

9	It's ready!	**VARIATION** You can leave out the egg whites.
TIP You don't need to use a strainer to mash the egg yolks (step 3), but it gives the sauce a smoother consistency.		**SERVING SUGGESTION** This is the classic sauce for calf's head, but it also goes well with crudités, steamed vegetables and cold meats (see recipe idea 12*).

SAUSAGE WITH GRAVY

YIELD: 1 SERVING • INCLUDES 1 BATCH OF MEAT GRAVY

✣ 1. Fry 1 large Toulouse sausage or a pork sausage of your choice.

✣ 2. Prepare the meat gravy as indicated in recipe 11, adding 1 tablespoon (15 ml) flour, about ½ cup water (125 ml) and 2 teaspoons (10 ml) mustard.

✣ 3. Serve with homemade mashed potatoes (see recipe idea 8*).

STEW WITH GRIBICHE

YIELD: 4 TO 6 • INCLUDES 1 BATCH OF GRIBICHE SAUCE

< 1. Gribiche can accompany hot, freshly prepared stew or cold leftovers.

13

CLASSIC MAYONNAISE

YIELD: ABOUT 1½ CUPS (375 ML) • PREPARATION: 15 MINUTES

1 egg yolk
1 teaspoon (5 ml) salt
1 teaspoon (5 ml) Dijon mustard
1¼ cups (310 ml) vegetable oil
1 or 2 teaspoons (5 or 10 ml) lemon juice
Ground pepper, to taste

FIXING A BROKEN MAYO:
A broken mayonnaise is one that's separated and does not have a smooth, even consistency. Fix by gradually whisking the broken sauce and remaining oil into a second egg yolk.

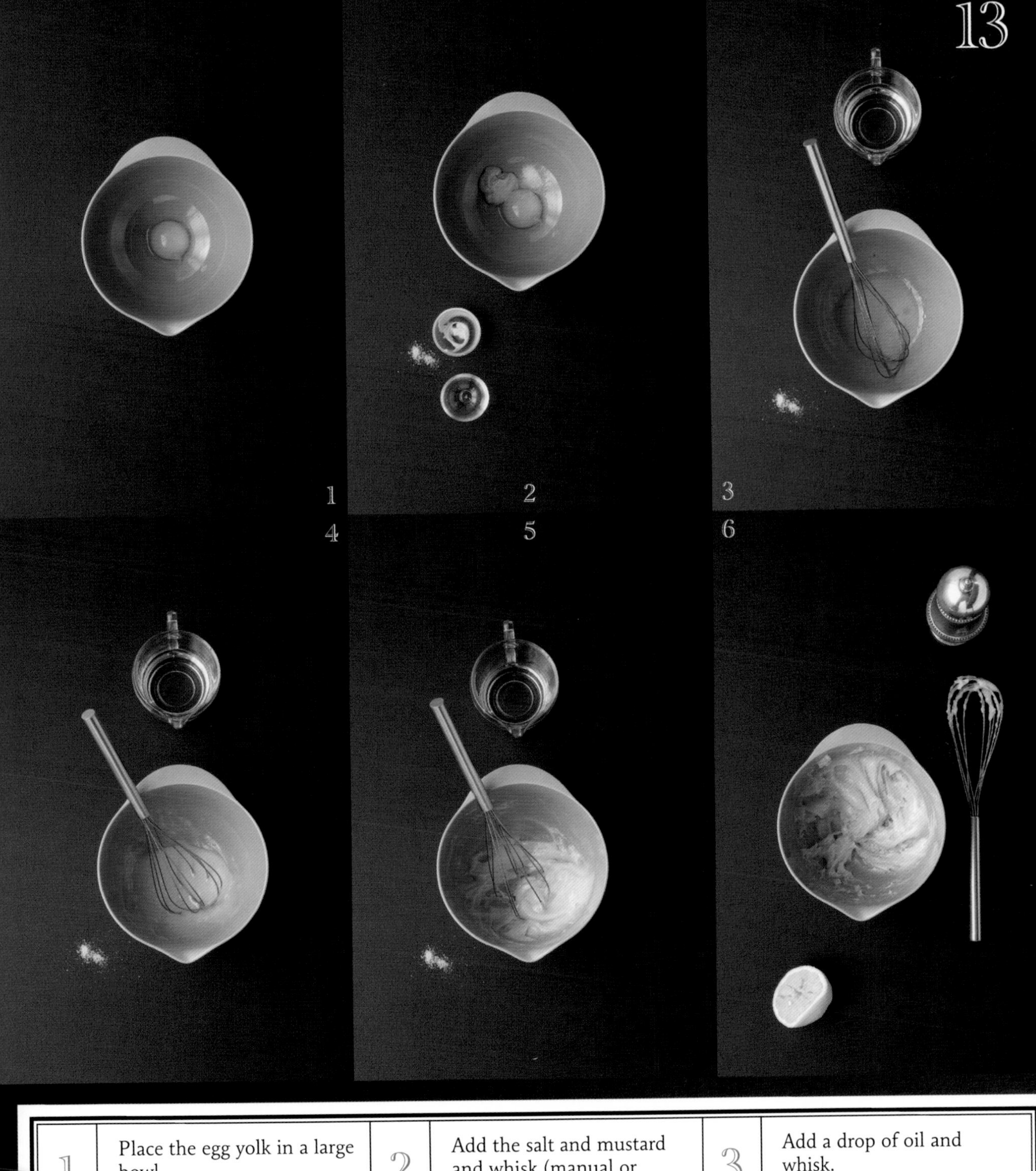

1	Place the egg yolk in a large bowl.	2	Add the salt and mustard and whisk (manual or electric) to combine.	3	Add a drop of oil and whisk.
4	Continue to whisk in the oil, drop by drop, until the mixture thickens.	5	Once you've added a third of the oil, gradually add the rest in a thin stream, whisking constantly.	6	Once the sauce is stiff, season with a little lemon juice and pepper.

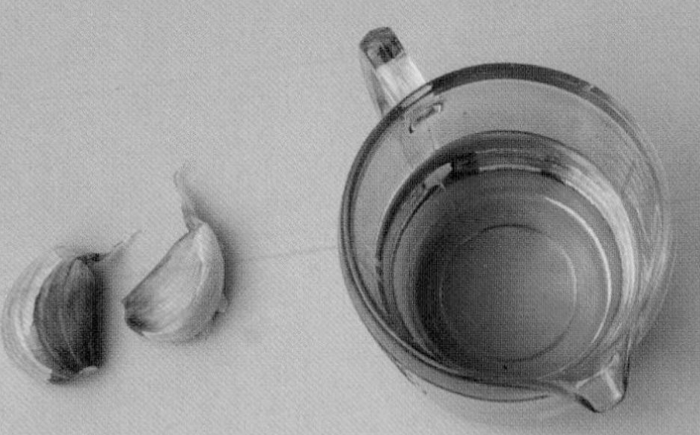

AIOLI

VARIATION OF CLASSIC MAYONNAISE

↞ 1. Crush 2, 3 or 4 garlic cloves (according to taste) with the salt when preparing a classic mayonnaise (see recipe 13).
↞ 2. Continue by following the method described in recipe 13, substituting olive oil for at least one third of the vegetable oil.

SERVING SUGGESTION: Cod (see recipe idea 72*) or cold roast beef.

GREEN GODDESS DRESSING

VARIATION OF CLASSIC MAYONNAISE

↞ 1. Prepare a batch of classic mayonnaise (see recipe 13).
↞ 2. Finely chop 3 sprigs basil, 3 sprigs flat-leaf parsley, 3 sprigs chervil and 3 chives. Mash 2 to 3 anchovy fillets in oil. Add the herbs and anchovies along with 2 teaspoons (10 ml) vinegar and 3 tablespoons (45 ml) crème fraîche or sour cream to the mayonnaise.
↞ 3. Taste and adjust the seasoning.

SERVING SUGGESTION: Leftover roast chicken.

16

MARIE ROSE SAUCE

VARIATION OF CLASSIC MAYONNAISE

⸎ 1. Add 3 tablespoons (45 ml) ketchup, 1 tablespoon (15 ml) Worcestershire sauce and 1 dash cognac or whiskey to a classic mayonnaise (see recipe 13).

⸎ 2. Gradually mix in the juice of 1 lemon.

⸎ 3. Taste and adjust the seasoning, if needed.

SERVING SUGGESTIONS: Beef fondue or shrimp (see recipe idea 16*).

TARTAR SAUCE

VARIATION OF CLASSIC MAYONNAISE

1. Finely chop 4 sprigs flat-leaf parsley, 6 to 7 capers and 3 to 4 cornichons or gherkins and add to a classic mayonnaise (see recipe 13).

2. Mix in 2 tablespoons (30 ml) ketchup and 1 teaspoon (5 ml) Tabasco sauce.

SERVING SUGGESTIONS: Cold meat (see recipe ideas 44* and 48*) or crudités.

13*

COLESLAW

YIELD: 6 SERVINGS • INCLUDES 1 BATCH OF CLASSIC MAYONNAISE

❖ 1. Wash and peel 2 carrots, ¼ red cabbage, ¼ white cabbage and 1 fennel bulb. Juice 1 lemon.

❖ 2. Finely slice all the vegetables, and chop 6 sprigs flat-leaf parsley.

❖ 3. Mix the vegetables and parsley with ½ teaspoon (2 ml) curry powder, 1 batch mayonnaise and 2 to 3 tablespoons (30 to 45 ml) lemon juice.

❖ 4. Season with salt, if needed, then add 2 tablespoons (30 ml) roasted pumpkin seeds.

SHRIMP WITH MARIE ROSE SAUCE

YIELD: 2 SERVINGS • INCLUDES 1 BATCH OF MARIE ROSE SAUCE

Mix two dozen small cooked shrimps, or a smaller quantity of larger shrimps, with 1 batch Marie Rose sauce, or serve the sauce separately, for dipping.

TIP: For a more substantial appetizer, garnish with avocado slices sprinkled with lemon juice.

ROUILLE

YIELD: 4 TO 6 SERVINGS • PREPARATION: 25 MINUTES

1 large pinch saffron threads
¾ cup (175 ml) dried bread crumbs (preferably homemade)

3 small dried chili peppers or ½ teaspoon (5 ml) cayenne pepper
1 pinch fleur de sel

3 garlic cloves
1 egg yolk
¾ cup (175 ml) olive oil
Table salt, to taste

1 2

3 4

1	Place the saffron in 2 tablespoons (30 ml) water (if you are making rouille to accompany a soup, you can use 2 tablespoons (30 ml) hot soup).	2	Mix the dissolved saffron with the bread crumbs. Add a little water if the mixture seems too dry; it should have the consistency of thick cream.	
3	Crush the chili peppers, fleur de sel and garlic in a mortar using a pestle or in a bowl using a wooden spoon.	4	Add the egg yolk and mix.	➢

5 6
7 8

5	Transfer the mixture to a large bowl. Gradually add the saffron–bread crumb mixture.	6	Mix well.
7	Gradually add the oil, as for mayonnaise, starting drop by drop.	8	Add the remaining oil in a thin stream, beating with an electric mixer.

9	Season with table salt, if needed. It's ready!	**SERVING SUGGESTION** This sauce goes well with fish soup with croutons. It's also good with poached cod (see recipe idea 72*) and seafood.

PASTA SAUCES

2

PESTOS

TOMATO SAUCES

RECIPE IDEAS

Some sauces are accompanied by a recipe idea, which is indicated with the recipe number and an asterisk symbol (*).

CLASSIC PESTO

YIELD: ABOUT ½ CUP (125 ML) • PREPARATION: 15 MINUTES • COOKING: 3 MINUTES

3½ ounces (100 g) basil (about 4 bunches)
¾ ounce (25 g) Parmesan
2 tablespoons (30 ml) pine nuts
⅓ cup (75 ml) olive oil, or a little more
2 garlic cloves

PRELIMINARY:
Wash and drain the basil, and pluck the leaves from the stems (discard the stems). Grate the Parmesan.

TIP:
If possible, place the blade of the food processor in the freezer for a few hours prior to making the pesto.

1	Roast the pine nuts over low heat in a dry skillet until lightly golden.	2	Blend all the ingredients except the Parmesan in a food processor.
3	Add the Parmesan manually, using a spoon or fork.	4	Taste, season with salt, if needed, and thin with extra oil if needed. It's ready! Serve as a dip with aperitifs (see recipe idea 19*).

PISTACHIO PESTO

VARIATION OF CLASSIC PESTO

⋄ 1. Using a mortar and pestle instead of a food processor, follow the method described in recipe 19, substituting pistachios for the pine nuts and arugula for the basil.

⋄ 2. Gradually add the oil, mixing with the pestle. You can make this recipe in a food processor, as explained in recipe 19.

SERVING SUGGESTION: Spaghetti (see recipe idea 20*).

WATERCRESS PESTO

VARIATION OF CLASSIC PESTO

⟡ 1. Proceed as indicated in recipe 19, substituting watercress for the basil and almonds for the pine nuts.

⟡ 2. Add the Parmesan and mix in using a fork.

⟡ 3. Taste and add oil if needed.

SERVING SUGGESTION: Spaghetti (see recipe idea 21*).

MINT PESTO

VARIATION OF CLASSIC PESTO

⟡ 1. Roast 1 tablespoon (15 ml) almonds in a dry skillet, stirring often to keep the almonds from burning.

⟡ 2. Using a mortar and pestle instead of a food processor, follow the method described in recipe 19, substituting mint for half the basil and roasted almonds for half the pine nuts.

SERVING SUGGESTION: Spaghetti (see recipe idea 22*).

RED PESTO

VARIATION OF CLASSIC PESTO

✧ 1. Peel 1 or 2 garlic cloves. Pluck the leaves from 1 large bunch basil. Rehydrate 1 ounce (30 g) sun-dried tomatoes in hot water. Grate ¾ ounce (25 g) Parmesan.
✧ 2. In a food processor, blend together the rehydrated tomatoes, garlic, basil and ¼ cup (60 ml) oil. Add a little of the tomato-soaking liquid if needed.
✧ 3. Add the Parmesan and adjust the seasoning.

SERVING SUGGESTION: Spaghetti (see recipe idea 23*).

19*

MOZZARELLA DIP

YIELD: 4 SERVINGS • INCLUDES 1 BATCH OF CLASSIC PESTO

⇐ 1. In a food processor, blend 1 batch pesto with 1 fresh mozzarella ball.
⇐ 2. Add a little mozzarella water, enough to obtain a creamy consistency.
⇐ 3. Use as a spread on bread or as a dip for breadsticks.

SPAGHETTI WITH PESTO

YIELD: 4 SERVINGS • INCLUDES 1 BATCH OF PESTO OF YOUR CHOICE

⪪ 1. Boil 12½ to 14 ounces (350 to 400 g) spaghetti in a large quantity of water.
⪪ 2. Once the spaghetti is al dente, drain and reserve a little cooking water.
⪪ 3. Mix the pasta and pesto, thinned, if needed, with the reserved cooking water.
⪪ 4. Serve with Parmesan shavings.

CLASSIC TOMATO SAUCE

YIELD: ABOUT 1 QUART (1 L) • PREPARATION: 20 MINUTES • COOKING: 50 MINUTES

3 sprigs basil
2 (28-ounce/796 ml) cans whole tomatoes
2 to 3 garlic cloves
3 tablespoons (45 ml) olive oil
Salt, & pepper, to taste
1 or 2 pinches sugar

PRELIMINARY:
Wash and drain the basil, and pluck the leaves from the stems. Chop the tomatoes.

1	Peel the garlic and slice as finely as possible.	2	Heat the oil in a sauté pan or skillet. Add the garlic and cook over low heat for a few minutes; the garlic should be cooked but not browned.	
3	Add the tomatoes. Simmer uncovered for 30 to 45 minutes, until the sauce is reduced and thickened.	4	Add the basil leaves, taste, season with salt and pepper, sweeten with sugar, if needed, and then taste again.	➢

5	Run the sauce through a vegetable mill.

TIP

You can also blend the sauce in a blender, but only do so briefly. You're not trying to obtain a smooth puree.

NOTE

You can keep the sauce as is and not pass it through the vegetable mill.

6	It's ready!	**SERVING SUGGESTION**
		Use this sauce with pasta, a classic lasagna or with veal or eggplant parmigiana (see recipe idea 24*).

VARIATION WITH FRESH TOMATOES

Ensure the tomatoes are fresh and tasty! You can peel them (after blanching) or not.

TIP

You can add 2 to 3 teaspoons (10 to 15 ml) butter at the end to make the sauce creamier.

ARRABIATA

VARIATION OF TOMATO SAUCE

✧ 1. Finely slice 1 small fresh red chili pepper and remove the seeds.
✧ 2. Proceed as described in recipe 24, cooking the fresh chili pepper at the same time as the garlic.

Instead of fresh chili pepper, add one large pinch of crushed red pepper flakes with the tomatoes.

SERVING SUGGESTION: Whole wheat pasta (see recipe idea 25*).

PUTTANESCA

VARIATION OF TOMATO SAUCE

❖ 1. Proceed as described in recipe 24, cooking 1 seeded and finely sliced fresh red chili pepper at the same time as the garlic.

❖ 2. Add 1 heaping tablespoon (15 ml) capers, 5 ounces (150 g) olives and 3 to 4 chopped anchovies in oil to the tomatoes. Do not season with too much salt because the anchovies are quite salty.

SERVING SUGGESTION: Long pasta (such as spaghetti) or short and hollow pasta (such as penne).

EXPRESS BOLOGNESE

VARIATION OF TOMATO SAUCE

⇠ 1. Chop 1 onion and fry for 6 to 7 minutes, until golden.

⇠ 2. Proceed as described in recipe 24, adding the garlic to the onions. Next add 9 to 10½ ounces (250 to 300 g) ground beef and cook.

⇠ 3. Add the tomatoes and ½ cup (125 ml) red wine, and then continue cooking as described in recipe 24.

SERVING SUGGESTIONS: Spaghetti or a classic lasagna with béchamel.

VODKA SAUCE

VARIATION OF TOMATO SAUCE

⟡ 1. Begin by preparing the sauce as decribed in recipe 24.

⟡ 2. Add ¼ cup (60 ml) vodka and add 1 pinch cayenne pepper to the tomatoes.

⟡ 3. Once the sauce has finished cooking, add 2 to 3 tablespoons (30 to 45 ml) sour cream over very low heat.

SERVING SUGGESTION: Fresh tagliatelle.

EGGPLANT PARMIGIANA

YIELD: 4 SERVINGS • INCLUDES 1 BATCH OF TOMATO SAUCE

∻ 1. Slice 3 eggplants and fry in a little olive oil. Season with salt, pepper and thyme.
∻ 2. Slice 2 balls of buffalo mozzarella.
∻ 3. In a baking dish, alternate layers of tomato sauce, eggplant and mozzarella. Finish with the tomato sauce and grate 1¾ ounces (50 g) Parmesan on top.
∻ 4. Bake in a 350°F (180°C) oven for 30 minutes.

WHOLE-WHEAT SPAGHETTI ARRABIATA

YIELD: 4 SERVINGS • INCLUDES 1 BATCH OF ARRABBIATA SAUCE

✣ 1. Boil 12½ ounces (350 g) whole-wheat, whole-grain or multi-grain spaghetti.

✣ 2. Drain the spaghetti and mix with hot arrabiata sauce and a handful of arugula.

✣ 3. Serve with Parmesan shavings.

ROASTED TOMATO SAUCE

⇝ **YIELD: ABOUT 3 CUPS (750 ML) • PREPARATION: 20 MINUTES • COOKING: 50 MINUTES** ⇜

1 garlic clove
1 anchovy in oil
8 plum tomatoes
2 to 3 tablespoons (30 to 45 ml) olive oil
Salt & pepper, to taste

PRELIMINARY:
Peel the garlic and crush or finely chop it. Finely chop the anchovy. Preheat the oven to 425°F (220°C).

SERVING SUGGESTION:
Use this sauce as a base for tomato soup (see recipe idea 29*).

1	Bring a pot of water to a boil. Put the tomatoes in a large heat-resistant bowl or a large saucepan and pour the boiling water over them. Peel the tomatoes and slice in half.	2	Arrange the tomatoes in a shallow baking dish and sprinkle the olive oil on top. Distribute the anchovy pieces and garlic over the tomatoes. Season with salt and pepper.
3	Roast in the oven for about 50 minutes.	4	Blend in a food processor or mash using a fork, keeping all the juice.

RAW TOMATO SAUCE

YIELD: ABOUT 1½ CUPS (375 ML) • PREPARATION : 20 MINUTES

1. Plunge 1 pound (450 g) fresh tomatoes in boiling water. Peel, seed and chop.
2. Mix the tomatoes with the leaves from 6 to 8 sprigs basil.
3. Add a little olive oil, salt, pepper and crushed garlic (optional).

SERVING SUGGESTION: Pour over pasta or use as a condiment with grilled meat or baked fish.

THREE-TOMATO SAUCE

YIELD: ABOUT 1½ CUPS (375 ML) • PREPARATION: 20 MINUTES • COOKING: 40 MINUTES

1. Place 9 ounces (250 g) cherry tomatoes on a baking sheet, sprinkle 2 tablespoons (30 ml) olive oil on top and roast for 40 minutes at 425°F (220°C).

2. Mix the roasted tomatoes and their juice with 9 ounces (250 g) fresh cherry tomatoes and 1¾ to 2½ ounces (50 to 75 g) sun-dried tomatoes, rehydrated or in oil and chopped.

3. Add 6 sprigs parsley, chopped, 2 tablespoons (30 ml) oil and a little salt and pepper to the tomatoes.

SERVING SUGGESTION: Pasta (see recipe idea 31*).

ROASTED TOMATO SOUP

YIELD: 4 SERVINGS • INCLUDES 1 BATCH OF BLENDED ROASTED TOMATO SAUCE

⋄ 1. Heat 2 to 3 cups (500 to 750 ml) vegetable or chicken stock, and mix with hot roasted tomato sauce. Add enough stock to obtain the desired consistency.

⋄ 2. Season with salt, pepper and a little Tabasco sauce.

⋄ 3. Place 1 tablespoon (15 ml) sour cream in each bowl. The soup can also be served cold, with or without croutons, garlic or rouille (see recipe 18).

PASTA WITH THREE-TOMATO SAUCE

YIELD: 4 SERVINGS • INCLUDES 1 BATCH OF THREE-TOMATO SAUCE

1. Cook 14 ounces (400 g) large pasta shells (or orecchiette or similar short pasta). Drain.
2. Mix with the sauce.

LEMON CREAM SAUCE

YIELD: ABOUT 1 CUP (250 ML) • PREPARATION: 10 MINUTES • COOKING: 10 MINUTES

1 lemon
3 tablespoons (45 ml) salted butter
1 scant cup (200 ml) light cream (20%)
Salt & pepper, to taste

SERVING SUGGESTION:
Try on fresh ravioli or fresh tagliatelle (see recipe idea 32*).

1 2

3 4

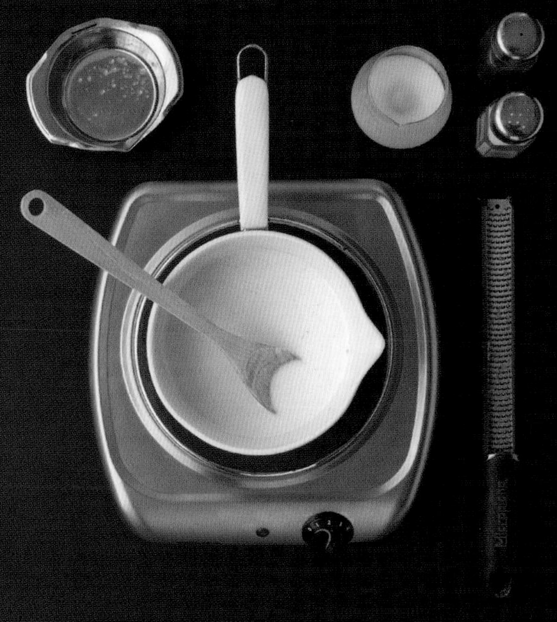

1	With the fine side of a grater, zest the lemon and then juice it.	2	Melt the butter in a small saucepan over low heat.
3	Add the cream, salt, pepper and the lemon zest and juice. Gently bring to a boil and cook for 2 minutes.	4	It's ready!

AGLIO E OLIO SAUCE

YIELD: ABOUT 3 TO 4 TABLESPOONS (45 TO 60 ML) • PREPARATION: 5 MINUTES • COOKING: 5 MINUTES

3 garlic cloves
3 to 4 tablespoons (45 to 60 ml) olive oil
1 pinch crushed red pepper flakes
Salt & pepper, to taste

SERVING SUGGESTION:
Aglio e olio (garlic and oil) is the sauce for late-night spaghetti (see recipe idea 33*). It's the recipe to prepare when you suddenly have hunger pangs and don't have anything fresh on hand. You can add bread crumbs browned in oil and chopped flat-leaf parsley for a crispier result.

1 2

3 4

1	Peel the garlic and slice it as finely as possible.	2	Heat the olive oil in a large saucepan.
3	Add the garlic and pepper flakes.	4	Brown the garlic very lightly over medium heat. The sauce is ready to serve, or you can thin it with a little pasta cooking water, if desired.

PASTA WITH LEMON CREAM SAUCE

YIELD: 4 SERVINGS • INCLUDES 1 BATCH OF LEMON CREAM SAUCE

1. Cook 1½ pounds (600 g) fresh tagliatelle or ravioli (such as spinach, ricotta or pumpkin) for 1 to 2 minutes, following the instructions on the package.

2. Serve with the warm sauce and freshly grated Parmesan.

SPAGHETTI AGLIO E OLIO

YIELD: 2 SERVINGS • INCLUDES 1 BATCH OF AGLIO E OLIO SAUCE

- 1. Cook 7 ounces (200 g) spaghetti. Drain.
- 2. Serve the sauce with the spaghetti.

You can strain the sauce (to eliminate the pieces of garlic, whose flavor will remain in the oil). Add a little pasta cooking water to thin.

CONTEMPORARY SAUCES

UNCOOKED SAUCES

COOKED SAUCES

RECIPE IDEAS

Some sauces are accompanied by a recipe idea, which is indicated with the recipe number and an asterisk symbol (*).

3

TOMATO SALSA

YIELD: ABOUT 2 CUPS (500 ML) • PREPARATION: 15 MINUTES • RESTING: 30 MINUTES

½ bunch cilantro
2 large, mature green onions or 1 small onion
4 ripe tomatoes (preferably on the vine)
Fresh red chili pepper, to taste
1 lime, juiced
1 dash tequila
Salt & pepper, to taste

PRELIMINARY:
Wash and drain the cilantro and pluck the leaves from the stems.

SERVING SUGGESTION:
Chicken skewers (see recipe idea 34*).

1 2

3 4

1	Peel and finely chop the onions. Soak in cold water.	2	Finely dice the tomatoes. Chop the cilantro leaves. Finely dice the chili pepper (remove the seeds).
3	Drain the onions and mix with the tomatoes, cilantro and chili pepper.	4	Season with 1 dash lime juice, the tequila, salt and pepper. Let rest at least 30 minutes in the refrigerator to allow the flavors to develop.

MANGO-ALMOND SALSA

VARIATION OF TOMATO SALSA

⇠ 1. Roast a handful of whole almonds (with the skins) in a 375°F (190°C) oven for 6 to 7 minutes. Chop with a knife.
⇠ 2. Dice 1 mango. Finely chop 1 small piece of fresh red chili pepper, 1 small onion and 6 sprigs cilantro.

⇠ 3. Mix all the ingredients and season with 1 dash lemon juice, 1 teaspoon (5 ml) olive oil, salt and pepper.
SERVING SUGGESTION: Blood sausage (see recipe idea 35*).

TOMATO-GINGER ROUGAIL

VARIATION OF TOMATO SALSA

⇠ 1. Mix 3 peeled and cubed tomatoes, 1 small piece grated ginger, 1 tablespoon (15 ml) sunflower oil, 1 finely chopped small fresh red chili pepper and a little salt.

⇠ 2. Blend in a food processor very briefly. You want the sauce's consistency to be more mashed than a traditional salsa, but it should not be a smooth puree. Ideally, use a mortar and pestle.

SERVING SUGGESTIONS: Grilled meats or baked fish.

CHICKEN WITH SALSA

YIELD: 4 SERVINGS • INCLUDES 1 BATCH OF TOMATO SALSA

1. Cut 4 chicken breasts into pieces and marinate in a little lemon juice, olive oil, salt and pepper for at least 1 hour or overnight, but not longer.

2. Slide the chicken onto the skewers and grill (in the oven or on the barbecue) for 15 minutes, turning once. Serve with salsa and bread (French stick or heated pitas).

BLOOD SAUSAGE WITH MANGO-ALMOND SALSA

YIELD: 4 SERVINGS • INCLUDES 1 BATCH OF MANGO-ALMOND SALSA

1. Fry 4 blood sausages in a little butter.

2. Serve with the salsa and a few dressed romaine leaves. Add a few new potatoes, if desired.

CHIMICHURRI SAUCE

YIELD: 4 SERVINGS • PREPARATION: 20 MINUTES • MARINATING: 3 HOURS

6 green onions
3 to 4 garlic cloves
½ bunch flat-leaf parsley
5 sprigs cilantro
Fresh red chili pepper or cayenne pepper, to taste
½ cup (125 ml) olive oil
¼ cup (60 ml) red wine vinegar
Salt & pepper, to taste

1 2
3 4

1	Peel and finely chop the onions and garlic. Wash and drain the herbs, pluck the leaves from the stems and chop the leaves. Finely chop the chili pepper.	2	Whisk the oil and vinegar (or shake in a jar).
3	Add the other ingredients, adjusting the amount of chili pepper to taste.	4	Let marinate for a few hours before serving. This sauce goes well with a good sausage (see recipe idea 37*).

GUACAMOLE

⇝ YIELD: ABOUT 1 CUP (250 ML) • PREPARATION: 15 MINUTES ⇜

1 ripe avocado
1 lemon (or lime), juiced
½ tomato

Fresh red chili pepper, to taste (or Tabasco sauce or cayenne pepper)
Salt & pepper, to taste

1 2

3 4

1	Slice the avocado in half and scoop out the flesh. Place in a bowl and mash using a fork, adding 1 tablespoon (15 ml) lemon (or lime) juice.	2	Finely chop the tomato (ideally, after peeling) and the chili pepper.
3	Mix the tomato and chili pepper into the avocado with a fork.	4	Season with salt and pepper. Add more lemon (or lime) juice, if needed. Guacamole is not only a dip, it also goes well with meat, fish and fried or scrambled eggs (see recipe idea 38*).

SAUSAGE WITH CHIMICHURRI SAUCE

YIELD: 4 SERVINGS • INCLUDES 1 BATCH OF CHIMICHURRI SAUCE

1. Grill 4 large Toulouse sausages, or the pork sausage of your choice.

2. Serve the sausages with the chimichurri.

MEXICAN BRUNCH

YIELD: 2 SERVINGS • INCLUDES 1 BATCH OF GUACAMOLE

1. Scramble 4 to 6 eggs. Season with salt, pepper and few drops Tabasco sauce.

2. Serve with the guacamole and good bread.

FRESH MINT CHUTNEY

YIELD: 2 TO 6 SERVINGS • PREPARATION: 15 MINUTES

1 bunch mint
2 large, mature green onions or 1 small onion
1 lime or lemon
¼ to ½ cup (60 to 125 ml) water
1 teaspoon (5 ml) sugar
1 large pinch salt

VARIATION:
You can add a little finely grated lemon zest or a piece of finely grated ginger.

1 2
3 4

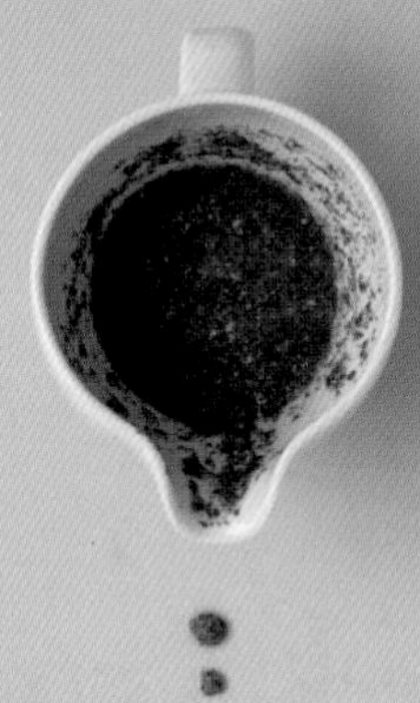

1	Pluck the mint leaves from the stems (discard the stems). Peel the onions and coarsely chop them. Juice the lime or lemon.	2	Blend all the ingredients with 1 tablespoon (15 ml) lime or lemon juice and ¼ cup (60 ml) water in a food processor.
3	Scrape the sides of the food processor and blend again, adding a little more water if needed in order to obtain a fine texture that's barely sticky.	4	Taste and, if needed, adjust the amount of lime or lemon juice and salt. Prepare this chutney for use the same day, as it does not keep well. Serve this sauce with shoulder of lamb (see recipe idea 39*).

CILANTRO-COCONUT CHUTNEY

VARIATION OF MINT CHUTNEY

In a food processor, blend 1 bunch cilantro (washed and drained), 2 tablespoons (30 ml) shredded coconut, 2 tablespoons (30 ml) coconut milk, 1 tablespoon (15 ml) sunflower oil, 1 small garlic clove, 2 to 5 tablespoons (30 to 75 ml) water, juice from 1 lime or lemon, 1 pinch cumin seeds, 1 teaspoon (5 ml) sugar and 1 large pinch salt, as described in recipe 39.

SERVING SUGGESTION: Large scallops (see recipe idea 40*).

CREAMY CHUTNEY

VARIATION OF MINT CHUTNEY

⇠ 1. In a food processor, blend 1 garlic clove, ½ bunch cilantro and ½ bunch mint (washed and drained) and 1 fresh green chili pepper (seeded).

⇠ 2. Blend with 1 teaspoon (5 ml) lemon juice and a little chili pepper. Season with salt and pepper to taste.

⇠ 3. Add ¼ cup (60 ml) Greek-style yogurt at the end by hand.

SERVING SUGGESTIONS: This sauce goes well with meat, fish and simmered dishes, or you can serve it as a dip.

39*

LAMB WITH MINT CHUTNEY

YIELD: 6 SERVINGS • INCLUDES 1½ BATCHES OF FRESH MINT CHUTNEY

1. Stuff 1 shoulder of lamb with garlic and sprinkle thyme, salt, pepper and 2 tablespoons (30 ml) olive oil on the outside. Roast in a 450°F (230°C) oven, allowing 20 minutes and then 15 minutes for every pound (500 g).
2. Lower the oven temperature to 400°F (200°C) after 15 minutes.
3. Serve the lamb with the chutney.

SCALLOPS WITH CILANTRO-COCONUT CHUTNEY

YIELD: 2 SERVINGS • INCLUDES 1 BATCH OF CILANTRO-COCONUT CHUTNEY

1. Sear about 20 scallops and 1 peeled garlic clove in a little olive oil over medium-high heat.

2. Season with salt and pepper. Serve with the chutney.

VARIATION: You can substitute shrimps for the scallops.

CUCUMBER RAITA

YIELD: ABOUT 1½ CUPS (250 ML) • PREPARATION: 15 MINUTES • RESTING: 30 MINUTES

2 sprigs mint
½ English cucumber or 2 to 3 small cucumbers
1 cup (250 ml) plain yogurt
1 lemon or lime, juiced
½ teaspoon (2 ml) cumin
Salt & pepper, to taste

PRELIMINARY:
Chop the mint leaves.

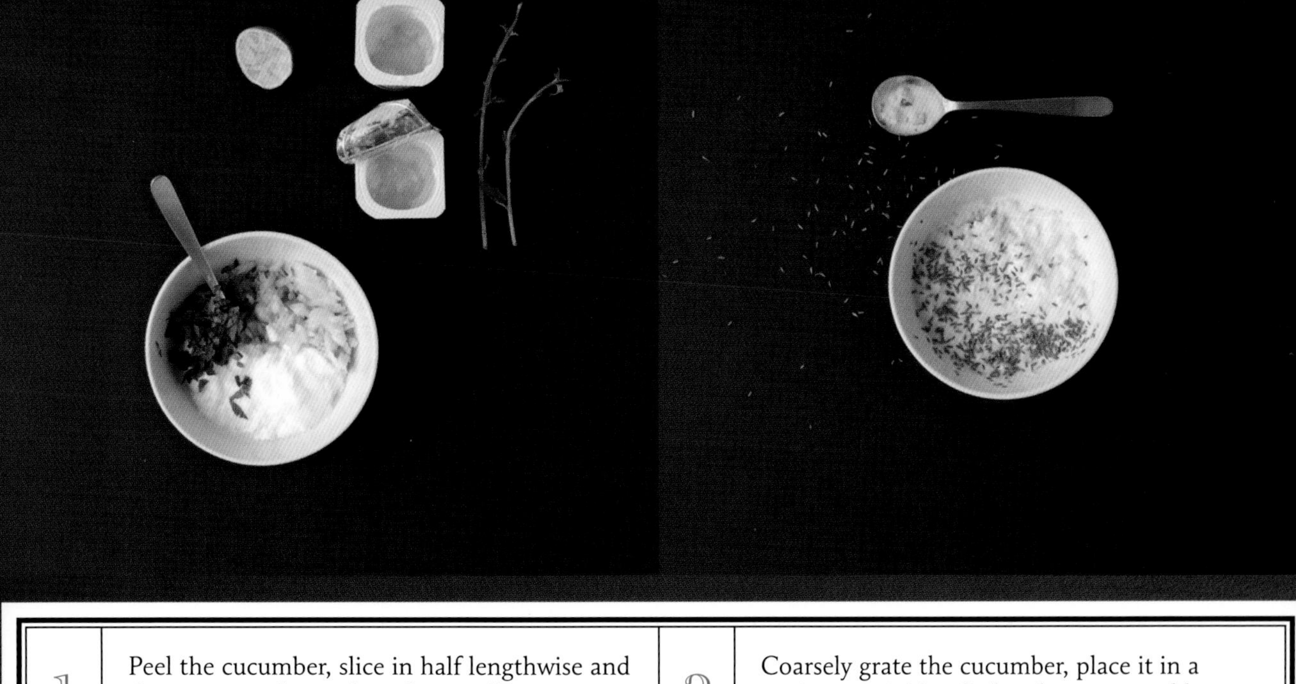

1	Peel the cucumber, slice in half lengthwise and then remove the seeds with a small spoon.	2	Coarsely grate the cucumber, place it in a strainer, sprinkle a little salt on top and let drain for 30 minutes.
3	Mix the drained cucumber with the plain yogurt, mint and a little lemon juice.	4	Sprinkle the cumin on top. It's ready! Serve raita with Indian dishes, such as lamb curry (see recipe idea 42*).

BELL PEPPER RELISH

→ YIELD: ABOUT 2 CUPS (500 ML) • PREPARATION: 15 MINUTES • RESTING: 1 DAY ←

1 red bell pepper
4 or 5 black olives (optional)
2 garlic cloves

1 tomato
Salt, to taste
Olive oil

SERVING SUGGESTION:
Serve with meat or fish (see recipe idea 43*), spread over bread or use in a lentil salad.

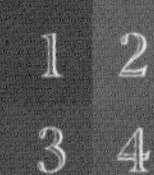

1	Wash the bell pepper. Remove the stem, seeds and white membrane and discard. Dice very finely.	2	Finely chop the olives and garlic (or crush the garlic in a garlic press).
3	Finely dice the tomato, but do not crush it.	4	Mix the ingredients in a glass jar and season with salt. Cover with oil, seal and store in the refrigerator for several days.

LAMB CURRY WITH RAITA

❧ YIELD: 6 SERVINGS • INCLUDES 1 BATCH OF CUCUMBER RAITA ❧

❖ 1. Gently brown 2 finely sliced onions. Add 1 crushed garlic clove, a little finely sliced fresh red chili pepper and some grated ginger. Add 2 teaspoons (10 ml) garam masala and 2 cans peeled tomatoes. Reduce for 30 minutes.

❖ 2. Reduce the heat to low and add ½ cup (125 ml) plain yogurt.

❖ 3. Gently fry 2 pounds (1 kg) lamb pieces until golden.

❖ 4. Put the lamb pieces in the sauce and cook for 30 to 45 minutes over low heat. Serve with raita.

SAUTÉED CALAMARI WITH BELL PEPPER RELISH

YIELD: 4 SERVINGS • INCLUDES 1 BATCH OF BELL PEPPER RELISH

1. Slice 14 ounces (400 g) calamari into rings.
2. In a hot oiled skillet, sear the calamari and cook for 2 to 3 minutes.
3. Serve with the relish.

ANCHOVY SAUCE

YIELD: 2 TO 4 SERVINGS • PREPARATION: 10 MINUTES

1. In a food processor, blend 3 anchovies, the leaves from 8 sprigs parsley, 1 teaspoon (5 ml) mustard, 4 to 6 tablespoons (60 to 90 ml) olive oil and 1 dash lemon juice.

2. Scrape the edges of the food processor's bowl, taste the sauce and add lemon, if needed. Thin with olive oil if needed.

VARIATION: You can substitute mint or basil for one-quarter of the parsley.

SERVING SUGGESTION: Veal cutlets (see recipe idea 44*).

CHOPPED ANCHOVY SAUCE

VARIATION OF ANCHOVY SAUCE

⧼ 1. Wash and drain 8 sprigs parsley, and pluck the leaves from the stems. Crush 1 or 2 garlic cloves.
⧼ 2. Chop the parsley leaves, garlic and 3 anchovies in oil together on a cutting board.
⧼ 3. Add a little olive oil to bind. You can also work with a mortar and pestle. However, do not blend in a food processor or blender.

GREEN SAUCE

⇾ **YIELD: 4 SERVINGS** • PREPARATION: 15 MINUTES ⇽

⇽ 1. Remove half the zest of 1 lemon and juice the lemon.

⇽ 2. In a food processor, blend ½ bunch chives, ¼ bunch flat-leaf parsley, ½ bunch chervil, ⅓ cup (75 ml) olive oil, 2 teaspoons (10 ml) capers and 1 tablespoon (15 ml) lemon juice.

⇽ 3. Check the seasoning and thin with olive oil, if needed.

SERVING SUGGESTIONS: This sauce goes with everything: cooked vegetables, grilled meats, fish, crudités.

GREEN SAUCE WITH ORANGE

VARIATION OF GREEN SAUCE

Prepare a sauce as indicated in recipe 46, substituting orange for the lemon. Use one-quarter of the zest and half of the juice.

SERVING SUGGESTIONS: Salmon fillets (see recipe idea 54*), lamb chops (see recipe idea 53*) and artichokes (see recipe idea 4*).

APPLE HORSERADISH SAUCE

YIELD: ABOUT 1 CUP (250 ML) • PREPARATION: 15 MINUTES • RESTING: 30 MINUTES

1 lemon
1 Granny Smith apple
2 sprigs flat-leaf parsley
¼ cup (60 ml) jarred grated horseradish
1 pinch sugar
Salt, to taste
3 tablespoons (45 ml) Greek-style yogurt, sour cream or whipped cream

PRELIMINARY:
Juice the lemon.

1 2

3 4

1	Peel and grate the apple. Wash and drain the parsley, pluck the leaves from the stems, discard the stems and chop the leaves.	2	Mix the apple with the horseradish, 1 tablespoon (15 ml) lemon juice, the sugar and a little salt. Cover with plastic wrap and let rest in the refrigerator for 30 minutes.
3	Add the yogurt or cream and adjust the seasoning with a little more salt and lemon, if needed.	4	Sprinkle the chopped parsley on top. Serve with cold leftover roast beef (see recipe idea 48*).

VEAL CUTLETS WITH ANCHOVY SAUCE

YIELD: 2 SERVINGS • INCLUDES 1 BATCH OF ANCHOVY SAUCE

1. Fry 2 veal cutlets in 2 tablespoons (30 ml) olive oil.
2. Season with salt and pepper, and then serve with the sauce.

TIP: You can marinate the cutlets in lemon juice, olive oil, salt, pepper, garlic and thyme before frying.

ROAST BEEF WITH APPLE HORSERADISH SAUCE

→ **YIELD: 6 SERVINGS** • INCLUDES 1 BATCH OF APPLE HORSERADISH SAUCE ←

Garnish the horseradish sauce with apple slices and serve with cold roast beef.

COOKING ROAST BEEF: Place the meat in a roasting pan, surround with onions or finely sliced shallots, pour a little water into the dish and cook in a hot oven. Test the roast with a meat thermometer to obtain the desired doneness.

MUSTARD SAUCE

YIELD: 2/3 CUP (150 ML) • PREPARATION: 15 MINUTES

3 sprigs dill
1 lemon
2 tablespoons (30 ml) mustard
1 tablespoon (15 ml) sugar

½ cup (125 ml) sunflower oil
1 pinch ground cardamom (optional)
Salt & pepper, to taste

1 2

3 4

1	Wash, drain and chop the dill. Juice the lemon.	2	Mix the dill with 1 tablespoon (15 ml) lemon juice and the all of the other ingredients, except the oil.
3	Gradually whisk in the oil.	4	Taste and add a little more lemon juice, if needed. This sauce can be served with salmon or tuna gravlax (see recipe idea 49*) or smoked salmon.

VANILLA SAUCE

YIELD: ABOUT 1 CUP (250 ML) • PREPARATION: 25 MINUTES • COOKING: 40 MINUTES • RESTING: 15 MINUTES

1 shallot
1 small carrot
About 20 raw large shrimps, with shells
1 tablespoon (15 ml) butter
7 tablespoons (105 ml) white wine (about a small glass)
3 or 4 sprigs thyme
1 bay leaf
⅔ cup (150 ml) heavy cream (36%)
1 vanilla bean
Salt & pepper, to taste

PRELIMINARY:
Peel and finely dice the shallot and carrot.

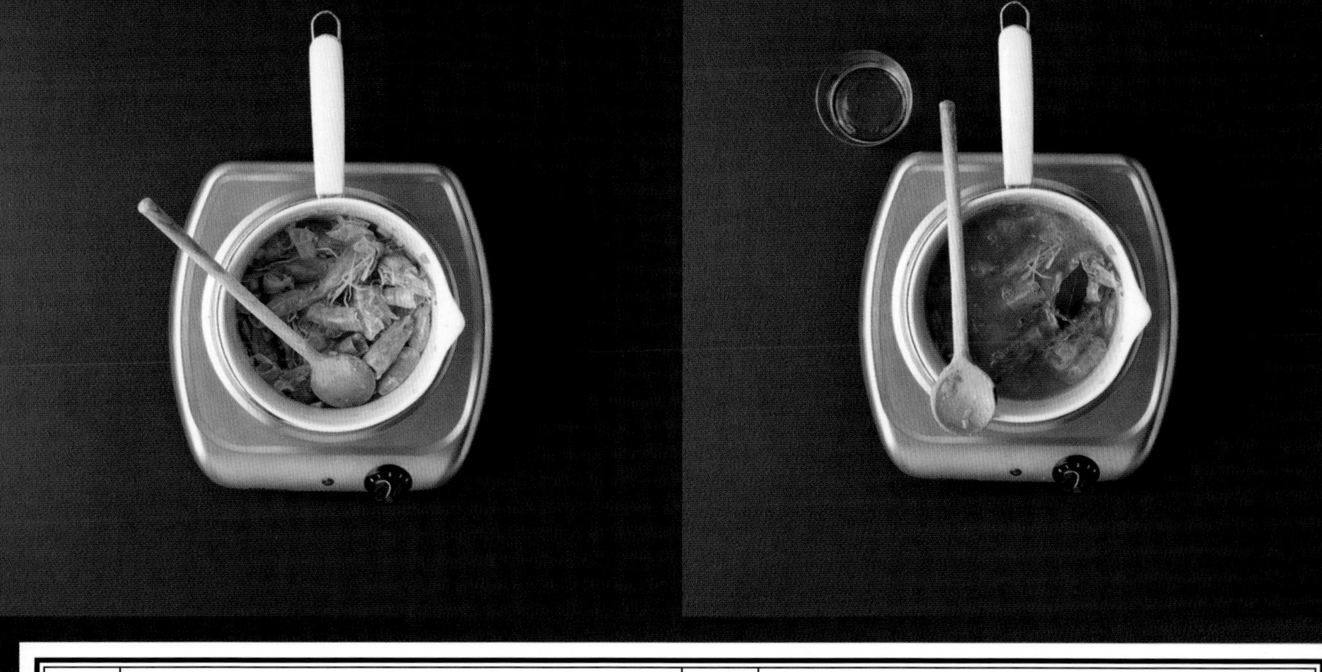

1	Peel the shrimps, reserving the heads and shells. Place the peeled shrimps in the refrigerator.	2	Melt the butter in a saucepan. Lightly fry the shallot and carrot for 5 to 6 minutes; do not let them brown.	
3	Add the shrimp shells and heads and cook, stirring, for 1 or 2 minutes.	4	Add the white wine then 1¼ cups (310 ml) water. Add the thyme and bay leaf, bring to a boil and then simmer for about 30 minutes.	➢

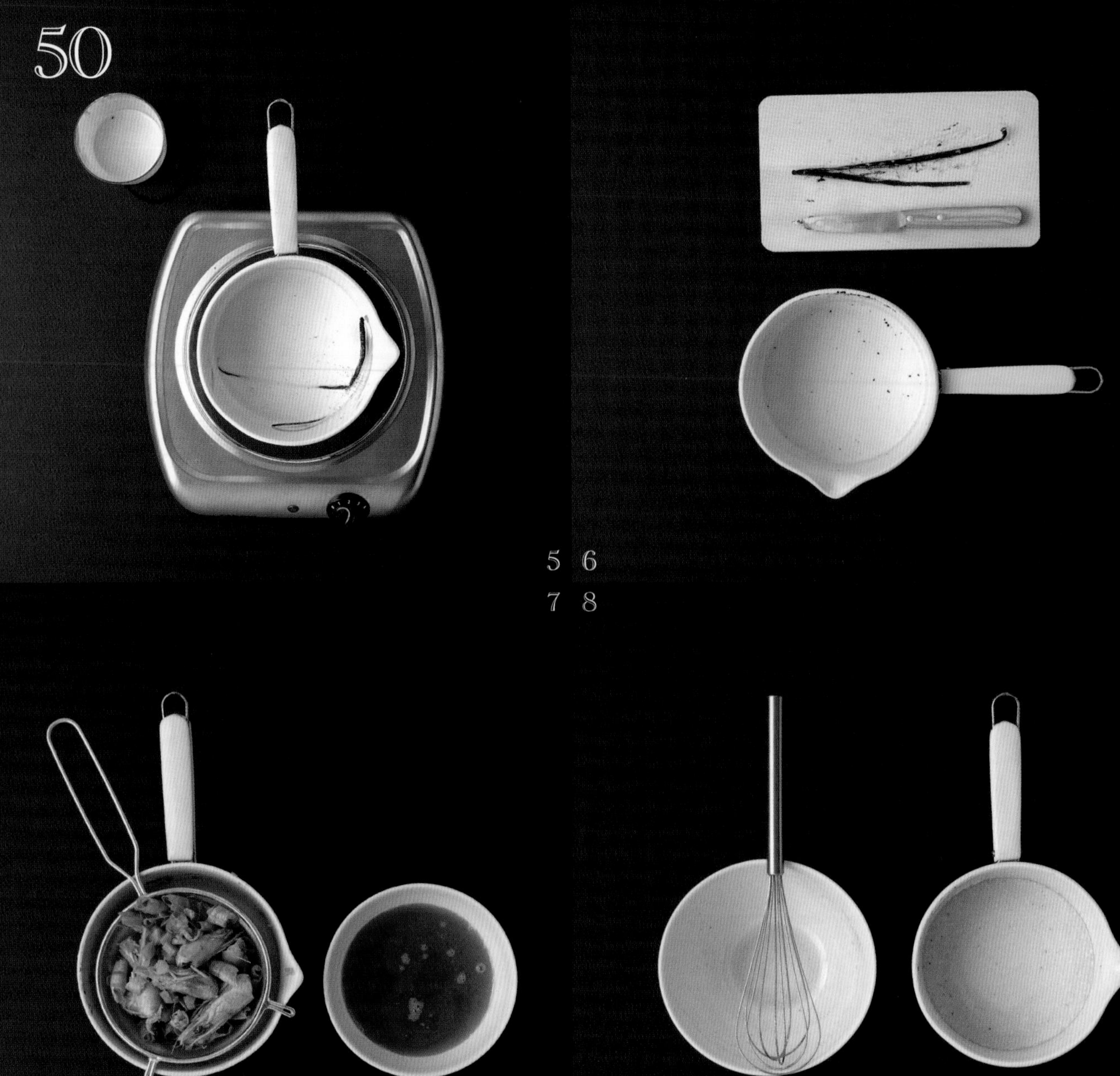

5	Gently heat the cream with the vanilla bean, which you've sliced in half. Once the cream is almost boiling, turn off the heat, cover and let infuse for 15 minutes.	6	Take the vanilla bean out of the cream and scrape the vanilla bean's seeds into the cream.
7	Filter the shrimp stock through a strainer, and discard the shells and heads.	8	Mix the fish stock and vanilla cream. Season with salt, if needed.

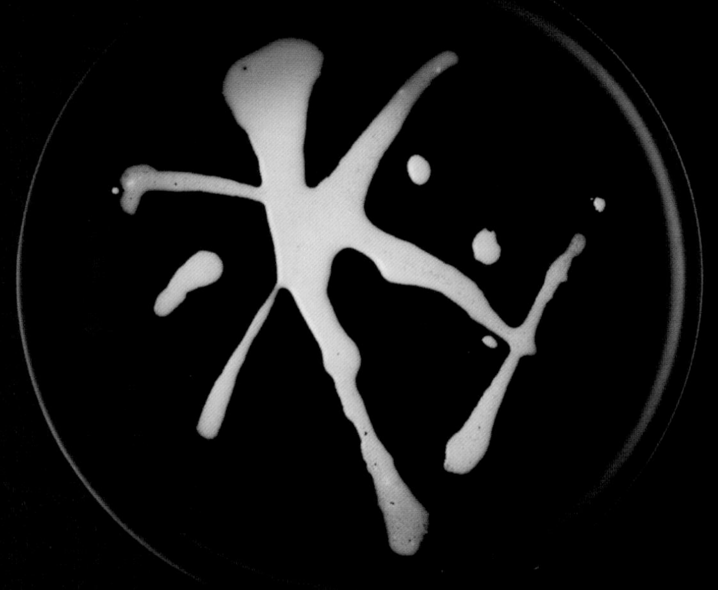

9	It's ready!

EXPRESS OPTION

If you don't have the time to shell the shrimps, you can use packaged fish stock. Allow ⅔ cup to 1 scant cup (150 to 200 ml).

SERVING SUGGESTION

This sauce goes very well with shrimps (see recipe idea 50*), scallops, delicate white fish (such as sole). You can also substitute vegetable or poultry stock for the shrimp stock and serve the sauce with veal.

FISH WITH MUSTARD SAUCE

YIELD: 4 SERVINGS • INCLUDES 1 BATCH OF MUSTARD SAUCE

1. Finely slice 4 fish fillets of your choice (such as salmon or bream).
2. Place the fish fillets in a dish, sprinkle a little lemon juice on top and lightly season with salt.
3. Stir gently and let marinate in the refrigerator for about 30 minutes.
4. Serve the sauce with the fish and garnish with dill, Swedish crackers or good toasted bread.

SHRIMP WITH VANILLA SAUCE

YIELD: 4 SERVINGS • INCLUDES 1 BATCH OF VANILLA SAUCE

1. Lightly fry the shrimps (the ones you set aside while preparing the sauce) in olive oil for a few minutes, until they turn pink and slightly golden. Stir often.

2. Serve the cooked shrimp and sauce as an appetizer. For a more substantial dish, serve with rice.

HOMEMADE KETCHUP

YIELD: ABOUT 2½ CUPS (625 ML) • PREPARATION: 20 MINUTES • COOKING: 1 HOUR 15 MINUTES

4 garlic cloves
1 onion
1 (½-inch/1 cm) piece ginger
1 red or yellow bell pepper
2 pounds (1 kg) very ripe tomatoes
½ cup (125 ml) red wine vinegar
1 pinch lemon zest
1 dash lemon juice
1 heaping teaspoon (6 ml) salt
7 tablespoons (105 ml) sugar
1 teaspoon (5 ml) mustard seeds
½ tablespoon (7 ml) peppercorns
¾ teaspoon (4 ml) coriander seeds
½ teaspoon (2 ml) cloves
1 small cinnamon stick

1	Peel the garlic, onion and ginger. Coarsely chop the onion, bell pepper and ginger.	2	Put the tomatoes in a bowl or a large saucepan and cover with boiling water. Peel the tomatoes and then coarsely chop.	
3	Place the tomatoes, onion, peeled garlic and bell pepper in a large sauté pan with half the vinegar and the lemon zest and juice. Cook for 15 minutes over medium heat.	4	Blend mixture in a food processor.	➢

5	Return the blended mixture to the saucepan. Add the remaining vinegar, the salt and the sugar. Assemble the mustard seeds, peppercorns, coriander seeds, cloves, cinnamon stick and ginger in a piece of cheesecloth. Tie with a piece of string and place in the tomato mixture. Cook slowly for 1 hour, until the sauce is sufficiently reduced and thick.	**VARIATION** You can vary the spices according to taste. **OPTION** If you find yellow tomatoes, choose a yellow bell pepper to make yellow ketchup!

6 Remove the spices. It's ready! Transfer to sterilized jars or store in a plastic container in the refrigerator (it keeps longer in sterilized jars). Eat once chilled, for example, with a burger and fries (see recipe idea 51*).

TIP

For sweeter ketchup, add a little more sugar.

HOW TO STERILIZE JARS

Carefully wash the jars in hot water, rinse and dry. Place in a 350°F (180°C) oven for 5 minutes, and then fill while they are still hot.

GADO GADO

YIELD: ABOUT 1 CUP (250 ML) • PREPARATION: 15 MINUTES • COOKING: 10 MINUTES

2 garlic cloves
1 small fresh red chili pepper
1 tablespoon (15 ml) sunflower oil
1 cup (250 ml) water
1 teaspoon (5 ml) brown sugar
Salt, to taste
½ cup (125 ml) smooth peanut butter

1 2

3 4

1	Peel the garlic and crush in a garlic press or finely chop it. Seed the chili pepper and finely chop it.	2	Heat the oil over medium heat, add the garlic and chili pepper and stir three or four times.
3	Add the water, brown sugar, a little salt and the peanut butter. Mix and let cook over low heat for 5 minutes.	4	The sauce is ready once it has thickened somewhat. Gado gado goes perfectly with vegetables and chicken (see recipe idea 52*).

BURGER

YIELD: 1 SERVING • INCLUDES HOMEMADE KETCHUP, TO TASTE

- 1. Lightly grill 1 burger bun.
- 2. Cook 1 hamburger patty.
- 3. Slice 1 sweet onion (or use onion jam).
- 4. Stack the burger: start with the bottom half of the bun, then add 1 or 2 slices of cheddar or other hard cheese, the ketchup, the meat, the onions, a bit of lettuce, pickles and finish with the top half of the bun.

VEGETABLES WITH GADO GADO

YIELD: 6 SERVINGS • INCLUDES 2 BATCHES OF GADO GADO

Serve gado gado as a dip for crudités, steamed vegetables (carrots, green asparagus, green peas, leeks, etc.) and chicken skewers.

CHICKEN SKEWERS:
Marinate 3 chicken breast fillets for 2 hours in lemon and olive oil. Slide onto skewers and broil for 10 to 15 minutes in the oven.

53

ROASTED ZUCCHINI SAUCE

✦ **YIELD: 2 TO 4 SERVINGS** • PREPARATION: 15 MINUTES • COOKING: 20 MINUTES ✦

2 sprigs mint
3 zucchini
¼ cup (60 ml) olive oil
Salt & pepper, to taste
1 teaspoon (5 ml) sugar
2 teaspoons (10 ml) red wine vinegar

PRELIMINARY:
Preheat the oven to 450°F (230°C). Wash and drain the mint, and pluck the leaves from the stems.

SERVING SUGGESTION:
Lamb chops (see recipe idea 53*).

1 2

3 4

1	Wash the zucchini and slice lengthwise.	2	Arrange the slices on a baking sheet and brush with 2 tablespoons (30 ml) olive oil. Season with salt and pepper. Roast in the oven for about 20 minutes.
3	Puree the cooked zucchini in a food processor with the remaining oil and the mint leaves, sugar and vinegar.	4	Adjust the seasoning, if needed, and thin with a little water to obtain the desired consistency — it should be a little runny (but not too runny).

CARROT SAUCE

VARIATION OF ROASTED ZUCCHINI SAUCE

1. Roast 6 carrots cuts lengthwise along with 2 shallots, 1 teaspoon (5 ml) cumin seeds and 1 pinch fennel seeds in a 450°F (230°C) for 40 minutes, until the carrots are tender.

2. In a food processor, blend with 1 tablespoon (15 ml) olive oil, 7 tablespoons (105 ml) vegetable stock and chopped parsley. Season with salt and pepper.

SERVING SUGGESTION: Salmon (see recipe idea 54*).

FAVA BEAN SAUCE

VARIATION OF ROASTED ZUCCHINI SAUCE

❖ 1. Cook 7 ounces (200 g) dried fava beans or 14 ounces (400 g) fresh fava beans. If using dried beans, cover with water and cooked uncovered over medium heat until tender. If using fresh beans, boil for 10 minutes.

❖ 2. In a food processor, blend the beans with 2 peeled garlic cloves, the leaves from 4 sprigs flat-leaf parsley and a little salt and pepper.

❖ 3. Add ¼ cup (60 ml) olive oil and thin with stock.

53*

LAMB CHOPS WITH ROASTED ZUCCHINI

YIELD: 2 SERVINGS • INCLUDES 1 BATCH OF ROASTED ZUCCHINI SAUCE

1. Brown 6 to 10 lamb chops in 2 to 3 tablespoons (30 to 45 ml) olive oil over high heat until golden.

2. Season with salt and pepper, and serve with a little freshly cut thyme and the roasted zucchini sauce.

You can thin the sauce with a little hot water to obtain the right consistency.

Lamb chops also go well with green sauce with orange (see recipe 47).

SALMON WITH CARROT SAUCE

YIELD: 2 SERVINGS • INCLUDES 1 BATCH OF CARROT SAUCE

1. Preheat the oven to 425°F (220°C). Place 2 salmon fillets on 2 sheets of parchment paper that are large enough to wrap around the salmon with extra space at the top.
2. Season with salt and pepper, and sprinkle 1 tablespoon (15 ml) olive oil on top. Fold the edges over and staple closed. Cook for 15 to 20 minutes.
3. Mix the sauce with a little stock or hot water to give it a runny consistency. Serve with the salmon.

These salmon fillets also go well with green sauce with orange (see recipe 47).

ROASTED EGGPLANT SAUCE

YIELD: 4 TO 6 SERVINGS • PREPARATION: 15 MINUTES • COOKING: 50 MINUTES

4 sprigs flat-leaf parsley
1 lemon
2 eggplants
⅓ cup (75 ml) olive oil
Small pinch harissa (optional)
Salt & pepper, to taste
½ cup (125 ml) Greek-style yogurt or 2 tablespoons (30 ml) tahini (sesame paste)

PRELIMINARY:
Preheat the oven to 450°F (230°C). Wash and drain the parsley and pluck the leaves from the stems. Juice the lemon. Wash the eggplants.

1	Slice the eggplants in half. Arrange in a baking dish.	2	Sprinkle with 2 tablespoons (30 ml) oil.	3	Bake the eggplant for 40 to 50 minutes, until tender.
4	In a food processor, blend the cooked eggplant with the parsley leaves, remaining olive oil, harissa, salt and pepper.	5	Add the yogurt or tahini and mix by hand.	6	Add a little lemon juice. Serve with roasted lamb or poultry or baked fish.

ARTICHOKE SAUCE

YIELD: 4 SERVINGS • PREPARATION: 10 MINUTES

4 sprigs flat-leaf parsley
9 to 10½ ounces (250 to 300 g) artichokes in oil, drained
½ lemon, juiced and zested

1 heaping teaspoon (6 ml) capers
Dash Tabasco sauce
Olive oil, for thinning
Salt & pepper, to taste

SERVING SUGGESTION:
This sauce is perfect with beef carpaccio (see recipe idea 57*).

1 2

3 4

1	Wash and drain the parsley, and pluck the leaves from the stems.	2	Place the artichokes, lemon juice, lemon zest, parsley leaves, capers and Tabasco sauce in a food processor.
3	Blend everything.	4	Taste, adjust the seasoning (salt, pepper, lemon juice and Tabasco sauce) and thin, if needed, with olive oil.

GINGER SOY SAUCE

→ YIELD: 2 SERVINGS • PREPARATION: 10 MINUTES • COOKING: 5 MINUTES ←

1 (1- to 1½-inch/3 to 4 cm) piece ginger
1 tablespoon (15 ml) neutral oil (such as grapeseed, canola or sunflower)
1 teaspoon (5 ml) sesame oil (optional)

¼ teaspoon (1 ml) brown sugar
2 tablespoons (30 ml) light soy sauce

PRELIMINARY:
Peel the ginger.

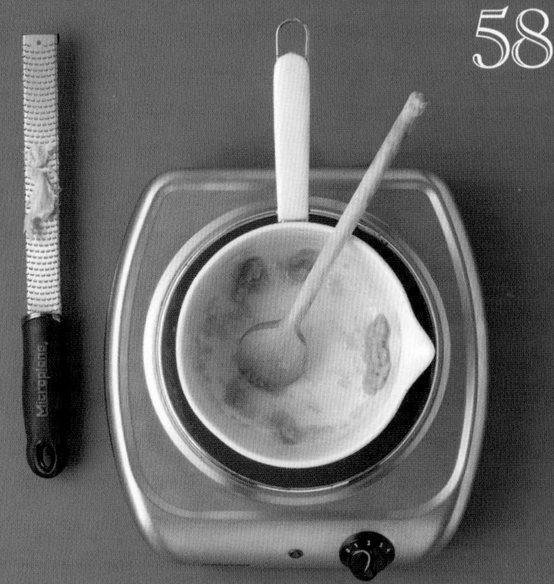

1 2

3 4

1	Heat the oils in a saucepan.	2	Grate the ginger over the saucepan and cook for a few minutes.
3	Turn off the heat and add the sugar and soy sauce.	4	Mix well. This sauce goes very well with steamed fish (see recipe idea 58*).

57*

BEEF CARPACCIO WITH ARTICHOKE SAUCE

YIELD: 4 SERVINGS • INCLUDES 1 BATCH OF ARTICHOKE SAUCE

1. Prepare a batch of artichoke sauce and thin with a little olive oil, as desired.
2. Slice a few Parmesan shavings using a vegetable peeler.
3. Serve 4 portions beef carpaccio with the sauce and Parmesan shavings.

FISH WITH GINGER SOY SAUCE

YIELD: 2 SERVINGS • INCLUDES 1 BATCH OF GINGER SOY SAUCE

1. Steam 2 servings of small vegetables, such as sugar snap peas, green peas and green asparagus.
2. Steam 4 bream fillets.
3. Serve the vegetables and bream with the sauce.

VARIATION: You can also serve ginger soy sauce with roasted summer vegetables and bream en papillote (i.e., wrapped in parchment paper).

TERIYAKI SAUCE

YIELD: ABOUT ¾ CUP (175 ML) • PREPARATION: 5 MINUTES • COOKING: 10 MINUTES

⅓ cup (75 ml) sake
⅓ cup (75 ml) mirin
⅓ cup (75 ml) light soy sauce
½ teaspoon (2 ml) sugar

SERVING SUGGESTION:
Strips of beef (see recipe idea 59*).

1 2

3 4

1	Place all of the ingredients in a saucepan.	2	Gently bring to a simmer.
3	Stir to dissolve the sugar. Reduce 5 to 7 minutes, until the sauce is a slightly thickened syrup.	4	The sauce is ready!

GREEN CURRY SAUCE

YIELD: 4 SERVINGS • PREPARATION: 20 MINUTES • COOKING: 10 MINUTES

½ bunch cilantro
3 garlic cloves
2 shallots
1 piece ginger
4 stalks lemongrass
2 or 3 fresh green chili peppers

2 limes
1 dash fish sauce
½ teaspoon (2 ml) black peppercorns
2 tablespoons (30 ml) sunflower oil
1⅔ cups (400 ml) coconut milk

PRELIMINARY:
Wash and drain the cilantro. Peel the garlic, shallots and ginger.

1	Cut off and discard any hard parts of the lemongrass. Seed the chili peppers. Cut away any hard steams or dead leaves from the cilantro. Zest 1 lime and juice 2 limes.	2	In a food processor, blend all of the ingredients except the oil and coconut milk to obtain a uniform paste.
3	Heat the oil in a large pot and cook the curry paste for a few minutes, stirring constantly.	4	Add the coconut milk and simmer for a few minutes. You can use this sauce to make chicken, vegetable or shrimp curry (see recipe idea 60*).

BEEF TERIYAKI

YIELD: 4 SERVINGS • INCLUDES 1 BATCH OF TERIYAKI SAUCE

1. Thinly slice 1 pound (500 g) beef tenderloin.
2. Sear in 2 tablespoons (30 ml) sunflower oil.
3. Top with teriyaki sauce and serve with 2 finely chopped large, mature green onions, including the green stalks.

CHICKEN & PUMPKIN CURRY

YIELD: 4 SERVINGS • INCLUDES 1 BATCH OF GREEN CURRY SAUCE

1. Cut 2 chicken breasts into pieces.
2. Rehydrate 1 handful dried wood ear mushrooms. Slice 1 small pumpkin into thin strips.
3. Add the chicken, mushrooms and pumpkin to the curry sauce and simmer. If you prefer, you can sear the chicken pieces separately in a little oil first and finish cooking in the sauce.

SALAD DRESSINGS

4

RECIPE IDEAS

Some sauces are accompanied by a recipe idea, which is indicated with the recipe number and an asterisk symbol (*).

61

CLASSIC VINAIGRETTE

YIELD: ABOUT ½ CUP (125 ML) • PREPARATION: 5 MINUTES

2 tablespoons (30 ml) red wine vinegar
2 teaspoons (10 ml) mustard
½ teaspoon (2 ml) salt
6 tablespoons (90 ml) sunflower oil or olive oil
Freshly ground pepper, to taste

1 2

3 4

1	Put the vinegar, mustard and salt in a bowl.	2	Mix with a spoon or fork until the salt dissolves.
3	Stir in the oil.	4	Season with pepper. This sauce is perfect with leeks (see recipe idea 61*).

LEMON ZEST DRESSING

YIELD: ABOUT ½ CUP (125 ML) • PREPARATION: 5 MINUTES

1 lemon
⅓ cup (75 ml) olive oil
½ teaspoon (2 ml) salt
Freshly ground pepper, to taste
1 teaspoon (5 ml) mustard

1 2

3 4

1	Zest about one quarter of the lemon using the fine side of a grater.	2	Juice the lemon.
3	Put 2 tablespoons (30 ml) lemon juice and 2 tablespoons (30 ml) lemon zest, the oil, salt, a little pepper and the mustard in a jar.	4	Shake vigorously. Serve with a mixed salad (see recipe idea 62*).

LEEKS WITH VINAIGRETTE

YIELD: 4 SERVINGS • INCLUDES 1 BATCH OF CLASSIC VINAIGRETTE

✧ 1. Cut off and discard any hard or damaged parts of 8 small leeks. Slice the leeks in half lengthwise.
✧ 2. Place in bowl or sink full of water, stirring to clean.
✧ 3. Steam until tender (about 10 to 15 minutes).
✧ 4. Refrigerate to cool and serve with the vinaigrette and a little grated licorice root, if desired.

SALAD WITH LEMON ZEST

YIED: 4 SERVINGS • INCLUDES 1 BATCH OF LEMON ZEST DRESSING

- 1. Wash and drain 1 head lettuce and 6 sprigs chervil.
- 2. Chop the chervil.
- 3. Steam a few romanesco broccoli florets then rinse under cold water.
- 4. Toss the lettuce, chervil and steamed romanesco. Serve with the vinaigrette.

RAS EL HANOUT VINAIGRETTE

VARIATION OF CLASSIC VINAIGRETTE

⊰ 1. Add ¼ teaspoon (1 ml) ras el hanout to the classic vinaigrette recipe (see recipe 61), at the start.
⊰ 2. It's ready!

OPTION : You can use curry powder (an Indian mixture) instead of ras el hanout (a North African mixture).
SERVING SUGGESTIONS: This sauce is ideal with cauliflower, avocado and artichokes.

HAZELNUT VINAIGRETTE

VARIATION OF CLASSIC VINAIGRETTE

⇠ 1. Place 2 tablespoons (30 ml) red wine vinegar, 1 teaspoon (5 ml) mustard, ½ teaspoon (2 ml) salt, 2 tablespoons (30 ml) hazelnut oil, ¼ cup (60 ml) olive oil and ground pepper in a jar.

⇠ 2. Shake vigorously. It's ready!

SERVING SUGGESTION: Avocado halves (see recipe idea 64*).

GARLIC VINAIGRETTE

VARIATION OF CLASSIC VINAIGRETTE

⟡ 1. Crush 1 garlic clove and ½ teaspoon (2 ml) salt in a mortar using a pestle (or in a bowl using a small spoon).

⟡ 2. Add 2 tablespoons (30 ml) lemon juice, 6 tablespoons (90 ml) olive oil and a little pepper.

VARIATION: Mash 1 or 2 anchovies with the garlic and salt for a sauce that is even punchier.

SERVING SUGGESTION: This dressing goes well with crudités, green salads and crisp-tender vegetables (such as broccoli and cauliflower).

CITRUS VINAIGRETTE

VARIATION OF CLASSIC VINAIGRETTE

⋄ 1. Mix the juice of 1 orange and 1 lime, 1 tablespoon (15 ml) honey, ½ teaspoon (2 ml) ground cumin, 1 small piece fresh red chili pepper, finely sliced and 1 tablespoon (15 ml) olive oil.

⋄ 2. Add the leaves from 4 sprigs cilantro, washed and drained. Mix well. It's ready!

SERVING SUGGESTION: A fall salad (see recipe idea 66*).

AVOCADO WITH HAZELNUT VINAIGRETTE

YIELD: 4 SERVINGS • INCLUDES 1 BATCH OF HAZELNUT VINAIGRETTE

Slice 2 very ripe avocadoes in half and serve with hazelnut vinaigrette.

VARIATION: Substitute walnut oil, pistachio oil or another nut oil for the hazelnut oil. It's best to combine an oil with a strong taste with an oil that is more neutral.

ROMAINE LETTUCE WITH CITRUS VINAIGRETTE

YIELD: 4 SERVINGS • 1 BATCH OF CITRUS VINAIGRETTE

✧ 1. Finely slice 1 red onion, place in the vinaigrette and marinate for 30 minutes.
✧ 2. Peel and dice 1 orange.
✧ 3. Arrange the leaves of 1 head romaine lettuce, washed and drained, the onion slices and diced orange on a plate. Dress with the vinaigrette.

CAMBODIAN VINAIGRETTE

YIELD: ABOUT 1½ CUPS (375 ML) • PREPARATION: 5 MINUTES

1. Mix ⅓ cup (75 ml) sugar, 1½ cups (375 ml) water, 1 tablespoon (15 ml) salt, 1 large garlic clove, crushed, and 1 dash lime juice until the sugar and salt dissolve.
2. It's ready!

OPTION: Add a dash of fish sauce.

SERVING SUGGESTION: Cambodian salad (see recipe idea 67*).

JAPANESE VINAIGRETTE

YIELD: ABOUT 1/3 CUP (75 ML) • PREPARATION: 5 MINUTES

1. Finely slice 1 green onion, and peel and grate 1 piece ginger. Juice 1 lemon.

2. Mix 2 tablespoons (30 ml) red miso paste, 1 teaspoon (5 ml) mustard, 1 dash water and 1 tablespoon (15 ml) lemon juice. Add ¼ cup (60 ml) sunflower oil then the ginger and green onion. Taste and add a little more lemon juice, if needed.

SERVING SUGGESTION: Japanese soba salad (see recipe idea 68*).

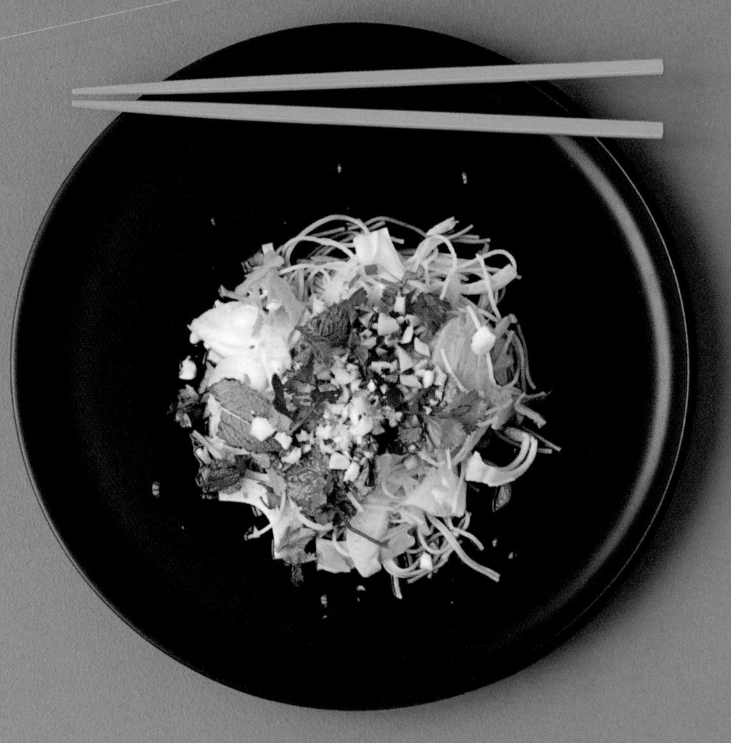

CAMBODIAN SALAD

YIELD: 4 SERVINGS • 1 BATCH OF CAMBODIAN VINAIGRETTE

1. Cover 1¾ ounces (50 g) cellophane (glass) noodles with boiling water, set aside for 10 minutes, drain and then rinse under cold water.
2. Finely slice 2 carrots, 1 fennel bulb, 1 cucumber and 1 fresh red chili pepper. Chop 6 sprigs mint and 4 sprigs cilantro.
3. Mix the raw vegetables, noodles and vinaigrette with shrimp or slices of cooked chicken.
4. Add the herbs, some ground roasted peanuts and a few sprouts (such as mung bean).

JAPANESE SOBA SALAD

YIELD: 4 SERVINGS • INCLUDES 1 BATCH OF JAPANESE VINAIGRETTE

⇠ 1. Boil 7 ounces (200 g) soba noodles.
⇠ 2. Wash 1 bunch arugula or watercress and remove any hard stems.
⇠ 3. Dice a bit of ham cooked on the bone.
⇠ 4. Toss the noodles with the dressing, and then add the arugula or watercress and ham.

HONEY-MUSTARD VINAIGRETTE

YIELD: ½ CUP (125 ML) • PREPARATION: 10 MINUTES

1 teaspoon (5 ml) mustard
1 teaspoon (5 ml) liquid honey
2 to 3 tablespoons (30 to 45 ml) lemon juice
1 pinch salt
Freshly ground pepper, to taste
6 tablespoons (90 ml) olive oil

1 2
3 4

1	Place all of the ingredients except the oil in a bowl.	2	Mix well.
3	Gradually add the oil, whisking.	4	It's ready! Serve this vinaigrette with chicken salad (see recipe idea 69*).

BLUE CHEESE DRESSING

YIELD: 1 SCANT CUP (200 ML) • PREPARATION: 15 MINUTES

3½ ounces (100 g) blue cheese (Roquefort, Gorgonzola, etc.)
1 dash Worcestershire sauce
1 tablespoon (15 ml) vinegar (red wine or cider)
⅓ cup (75 ml) olive oil
2 sprigs chervil (optional)
Freshly ground pepper, to taste

TIP: If you prefer to blend this dressing with a food processor, follow the method described here, but set aside a quarter of the cheese, crumble it and then mix it in by hand at the end.

1 2

3 4

1	Mash the cheese with a fork.	2	Add the Worcestershire sauce and vinegar.
3	Gradually add the oil, whisking.	4	Wash and chop the chervil, and add it and the pepper. Use this dressing on a winter salad (see recipe idea 70*).

CHICKEN WITH HONEY-MUSTARD VINAIGRETTE

YIELD: 4 SERVINGS • INCLUDES 1 BATCH OF HONEY-MUSTARD VINAIGRETTE

- 1. Cook a few potatoes.
- 2. Wash and drain 1 head romaine lettuce.
- 3. Mix the lettuce, vinaigrette and cooked potatoes with a few pieces of cold leftover roast chicken.

WINTER SALAD WITH BLUE CHEESE DRESSING

YIELD: 4 SERVINGS • INCLUDES 1 BATCH OF BLUE CHEESE DRESSING

- 1. Brown 6 to 8 slices of pancetta or bacon.
- 2. Wash and drain winter lettuces of your choice (such as radicchio, baby spinach, Belgian endive, curly endive or chicory).
- 3. Separate the lettuce leaves from the heads and cut any large leaves, if needed.
- 4. Arrange the lettuce leaves and cooked pancetta on a plate.
- 5. Dress with blue cheese dressing.

71

CAESAR DRESSING

YIELD: ABOUT ¾ CUP (175) ML • PREPARATION: 15 MINUTES

1 garlic clove
2 anchovies in oil
1 lemon
1 egg yolk
1 dash Worcestershire sauce
1 teaspoon (5 ml) mustard
⅔ cup (150 ml) olive oil

1 2

3 4

1	Peel then crush the garlic. Finely chop the anchovies. Juice the lemon.	2	Whisk together the egg, garlic, anchovies, Worcestershire sauce, mustard and 1 tablespoon (15 ml) lemon juice.
3	Gradually add the oil.	4	The dressing should be thick but still runny. This dressing is an essential element of a good Caesar salad (see recipe idea 71*).

CUBAN MOJO DRESSING

YIELD: ½ CUP (125 ML) • PREPARATION: 10 MINUTES • COOKING: 5 MINUTES

2 to 3 limes
3 to 4 garlic cloves
¼ cup (60 ml) olive oil
1 pinch ground cumin
Salt & pepper, to taste

PRELIMINARY:
Juice the limes. Peel and finely slice the garlic (or crush in a garlic press).

1 2

3 4

1	Heat the oil in a saucepan, add the garlic and brown very lightly. Let cool.	2	Add 5 to 6 tablespoons (75 to 90 ml) lemon juice and the cumin, salt and pepper to the garlic and oil.
3	Bring to a boil then turn off the heat.	4	Let cool. It's ready! Serve with cod (see recipe idea 72*).

71*

CAESAR SALAD

YIELD: 4 SERVINGS • INCLUDES 1 BATCH OF CAESAR DRESSING

1. Wash and drain 1 head romaine lettuce.
2. Toss with the dressing, a few croutons and some Parmesan shavings.

VARIATION: You can add sautéed chicken breasts or slices of avocado sprinkled with lemon juice.

COD WITH CUBAN MOJO DRESSING

YIELD: 4 SERVINGS • INCLUDES 1 BATCH OF CUBAN MOJO DRESSING

⋄ 1. Soak 1¾ pounds (800 g) salted cod for 24 hours to remove the salt, changing the water three times. Slice into strips.

⋄ 2. Serve with the dressing and and a few small ripe tomatoes.

VARIATIONS: You can poach the cod, if desired. Cod also goes well with aioli (see recipe 14).

FOAMS

5

RECIPE IDEAS

Some sauces are accompanied by a recipe idea, which is indicated with the recipe number and an asterisk symbol (*).

MUSHROOM FOAM

YIELD: 4 SERVINGS • PREPARATION: 25 MINUTES • COOKING: 7 MINUTES • RESTING: 15 MINUTES

14 ounces (400 g) chanterelles, porcini or other mushrooms
2 tablespoons (30 ml) butter
⅔ cup (150 ml) heavy cream (36%)
Salt & pepper, to taste
¾ teaspoon (4 ml) unflavored gelatin powder or 1 gelatin sheet

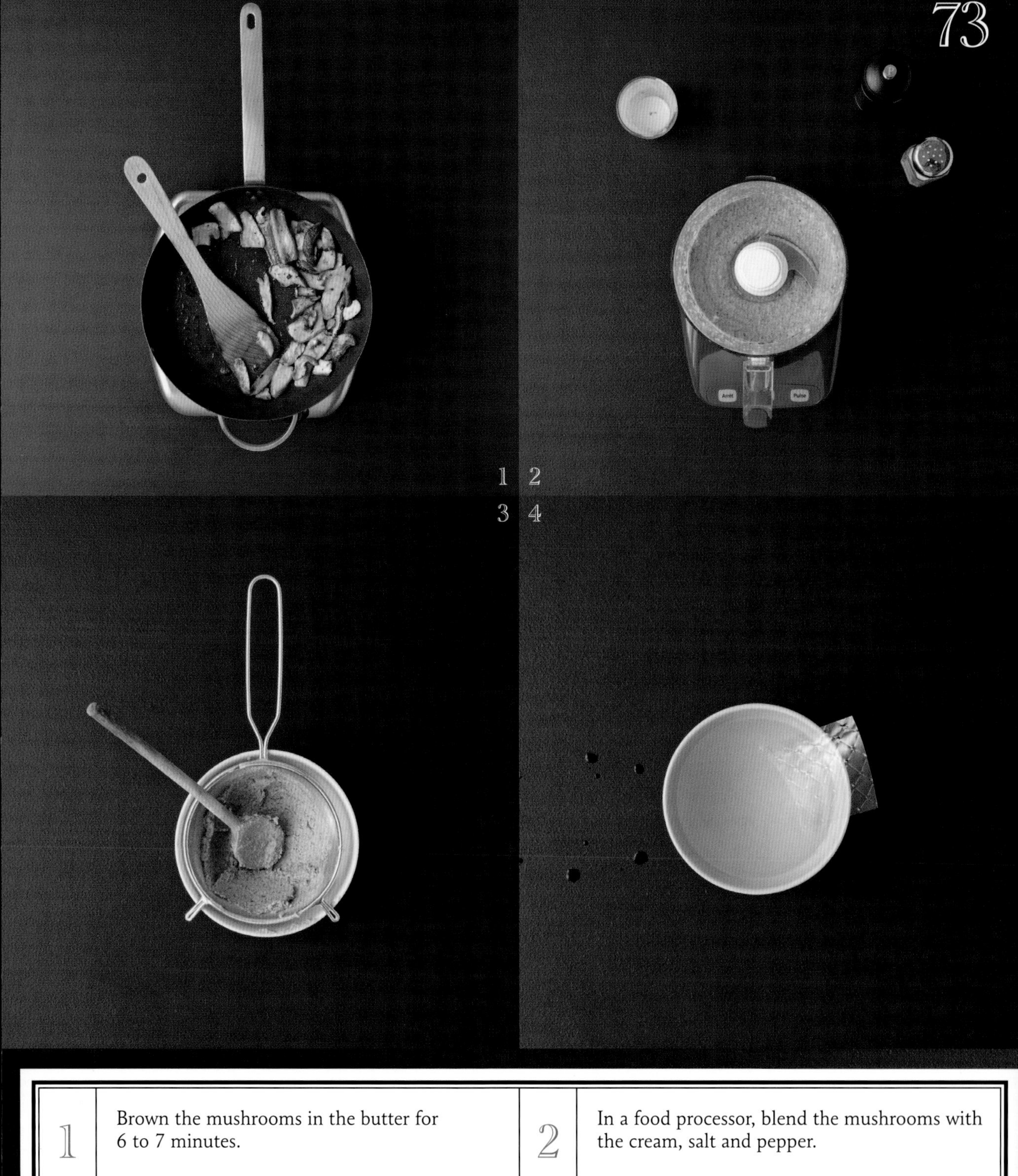

1	Brown the mushrooms in the butter for 6 to 7 minutes.	2	In a food processor, blend the mushrooms with the cream, salt and pepper.
3	Pass the mixture through a fine strainer.	4	Dissolve the gelatin in a little cold water (if using sheet gelatin, soak in cold water until softened then drain). ➢

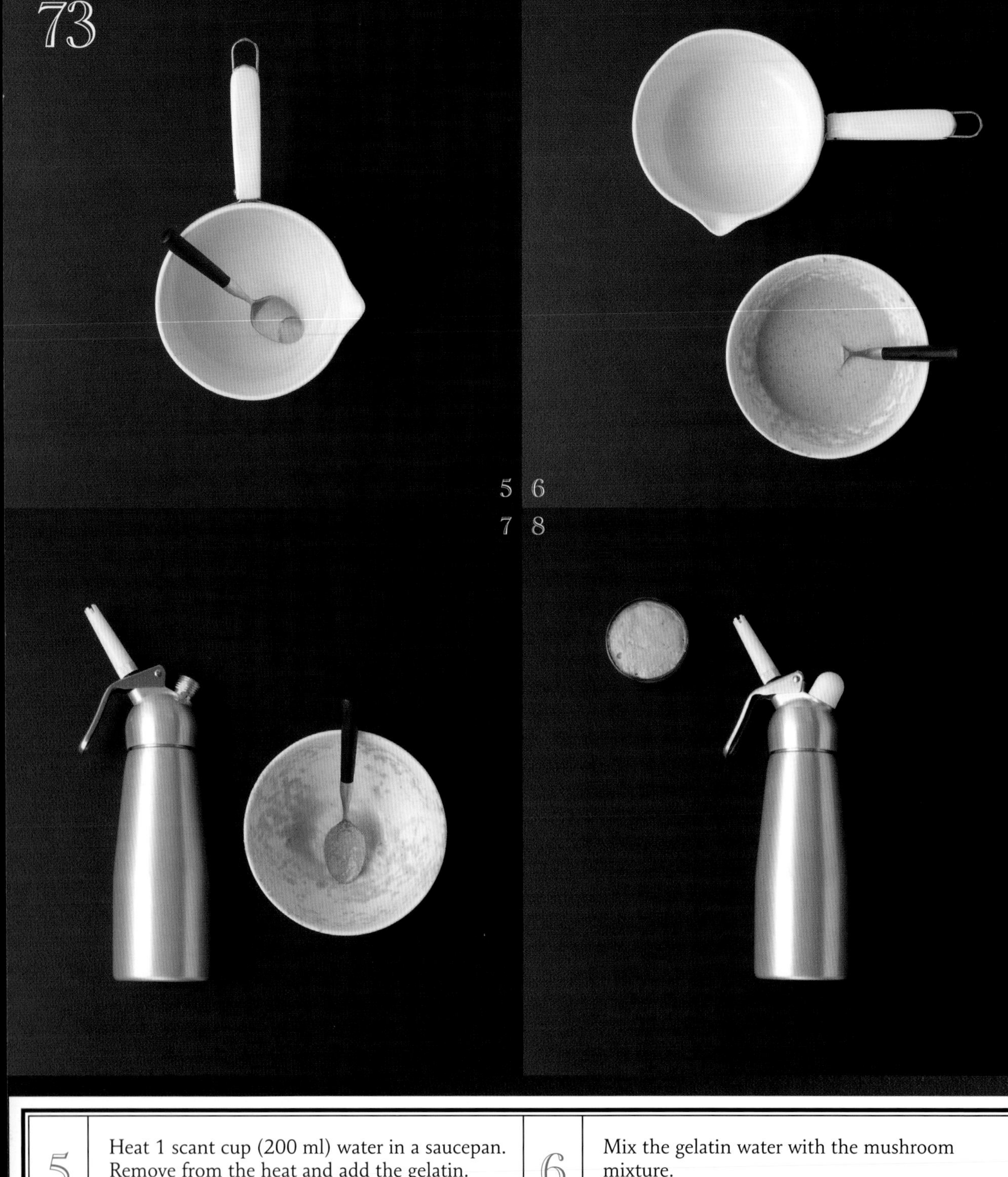

5 6
7 8

5	Heat 1 scant cup (200 ml) water in a saucepan. Remove from the heat and add the gelatin.	6	Mix the gelatin water with the mushroom mixture.
7	Place the mushroom mixture in a siphon (a pressurized canister) and insert the gas cartridge.	8	Shake then remove the cartridge. Let rest for 15 minutes at room temperature.

9	Make the foam.	**SERVING SUGGESTION** This foam is perfect with a mushroom velouté (a thick, velvety sauce) or fried chanterelles (see recipe idea 73*).

COCONUT FOAM

YIELD: $1\frac{2}{3}$ CUPS (400 ML) • PREPARATION: 25 MINUTES • RESTING: 30 MINUTES

1 lime
Fresh ginger, to taste
$1\frac{2}{3}$ cups (400 ml) coconut milk

$\frac{3}{4}$ teaspoon (4 ml) unflavored gelatin dissolved in 7 tablespoons (105 ml) boiling water

Chili powder or finely chopped fresh red chili pepper, to taste
Salt & pepper, to taste

1 2
3 4

1	Zest the lime and peel the ginger.	2	In a food processor, blend the zest and ginger with the coconut milk, gelatin and chili pepper. Season with salt and pepper.
3	Place the mixture in a siphon, shake and let rest for about 30 minutes in the refrigerator or 10 minutes in the freezer, shaking occasionally.	4	Shake the chilled siphon and squeeze to make the foam. Serve with red lentil soup (see recipe idea 74*).

73*

FRIED CHANTERELLES

YIELD: 4 SERVINGS • INCLUDES 1 BATCH OF MUSHROOM FOAM

1. Brown 1½ pounds (600 g) chanterelles in 2 tablespoons (30 ml) butter.

2. Serve with mushroom foam and some chives.

LENTIL SOUP

YIELD: 4 SERVINGS • INCLUDES 1 BATCH OF COCONUT FOAM

1. Put 7 ounces (200 g) red lentils, 3 cardamom pods, 1 cinnamon stick, 1 pinch ground cumin, 1 pinch turmeric, 14 ounces (400 g) peeled tomatoes, 1 chopped onion and 1 chopped garlic clove in a large saucepan.
2. Cover with cold water and cook for 20 to 25 minutes.
3. Remove the cardamom pods and cinnamon stick, and then blend in a food processor.
4. Serve the soup with a dollop of coconut foam.

FOIE GRAS FOAM

→ YIELD: 4 SERVINGS • PREPARATION: 15 MINUTES • RESTING: 30 MINUTES ←

2 slices whole semi-cooked foie gras
Salt & pepper, to taste
1 dash cognac

¾ teaspoon (4 ml) unflavored gelatin powder dissolved in 1 cup (250 ml) boiling water

TIP:
Allow the gelatin water to cool before blending if the food processor's bowl is not made of glass.

1 2

3 4

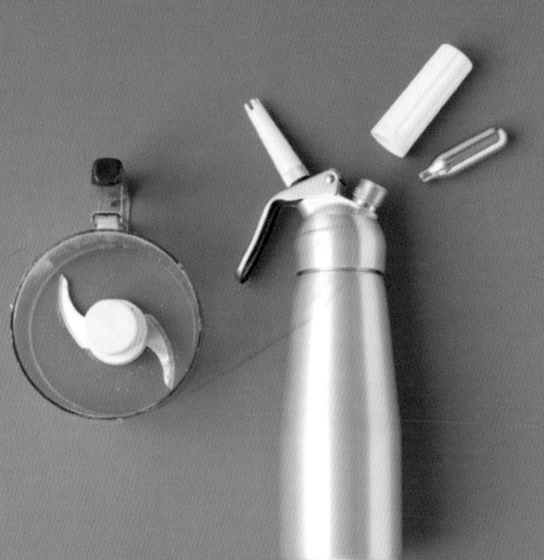

1	Blend the foie gras, salt, pepper and cognac in a food processor.	2	Add the gelatin water.
3	Pour into a siphon, insert the gas cartridge and then shake. Remove the cartridge.	4	Let rest for about 30 minutes in the refrigerator, shaking regularly. Discharge the foam. Serve with potato-leek soup (see recipe idea 75*).

HAM FOAM

YIELD: 4 SERVINGS • PREPARATION: 25 MINUTES • RESTING: 30 MINUTES

3½ ounces (100 g) Serrano ham
¾ teaspoon (4 ml) unflavored gelatin powder dissolved in 1 cup (250 ml) boiling water

Pepper, to taste

1 2
3 4

1	In a food processor, blend the ham with the gelatin water and pepper.	2	Pass the mixture through a strainer. Season with pepper, if desired.
3	Place in a siphon and shake. Let cool for about 30 minutes in the refrigerator or 10 minutes in the freezer, shaking occasionally.	4	Shake one last time and discharge the foam. Serve with pumpkin soup (see recipe idea 76*).

75*

POTATO-LEEK SOUP

YIELD: 4 SERVINGS • INCLUDES 1 BATCH OF FOIE GRAS FOAM

⇠ 1. Lightly brown 1 onion in 1 tablespoon (15 ml) butter.
⇠ 2. Add 2 peeled and diced potatoes then 4 to 5 leeks, cleaned and sliced.
⇠ 3. Add 2 cups (½ L) poultry or vegetable stock, and cook for about 25 minutes.
⇠ 4. Blend the vegetables in a food processor. Adjust the seasoning, if needed, and serve with the foam.

PUMPKIN SOUP

YIELD: 4 SERVINGS • INCLUDES 1 BATCH OF HAM FOAM

⇠ 1. Lightly brown 1 chopped onion in 1 tablespoon (15 ml) butter.

⇠ 2. Add 2 peeled and diced potatoes then 1 large slice pumpkin, peeled and cut into pieces.

⇠ 3. Add 2 cups (½ L) chicken or vegetable stock and cook for about 25 minutes.

⇠ 4. Blend in a food processor or grind in a vegetable mill. Adjust the seasoning, if needed. Serve with the foam.

SWEET SAUCES

6

RECIPE IDEAS

Some sauces are accompanied by a recipe idea, which is indicated with the recipe number and an asterisk symbol (*).

NOUGAT FOAM

YIELD: ABOUT ¾ CUP (175 ML) • PREPARATION: 25 MINUTES • RESTING: 30 MINUTES

3½ ounces (100 g) soft nougat, preferably turrón
¾ teaspoon (4 ml) unflavored gelatin powder dissolved in ½ cup (125 ml) boiling water

PRODUCT INFO:
Take care with this recipe. Choose soft Spanish "jijona" nougat, which melts in your mouth (hard nougat, Montelimar nougat and Italian nougat are not suitable). You can find turrón nougat in specialty stores, gourmet food stores and online.

77

1	Blend the nougat in a food pocessor.	2	Add the gelatin water. Blend.
3	Pass the mixture through a strainer. Place it in a siphon, shake and let rest for about 30 minutes in the refrigerator or 10 minutes in the freezer, shaking occasionally.	4	Shake and squeeze to discharge the foam. You can serve this foam with homemade ice cream (see recipe idea 77*).

WHIPPED CREAM

YIELD: ABOUT 3⅓ CUPS (800 ML) • PREPARATION: 10 MINUTES

1 dash rum (optional)
2 tablespoons (30 ml) sugar, more or less, to taste
1 drop vanilla extract
1⅔ cups (400 ml) heavy cream (36%), chilled (straight from the refrigerator)

1 2

3 4

1	Mix the rum, sugar and vanilla. Stir until the sugar dissolves.	2	Mix with the cream.
3	Place in a siphon and insert the gas cartridge.	4	Shake and squeeze to discharge the whipped cream. Serve with crepes (see recipe idea 78*).

CARAMEL SAUCE

YIELD: 4 TO 6 SERVINGS • PREPARATION: 20 MINUTES

⅞ cup (200 ml) sugar
5 tablespoons (75 ml) water
½ cup (125 ml) unsalted (or salted) butter, cut into pieces
1 dash whiskey
½ cup (125 ml) crème fraîche or sour cream
1 pinch salt
2 to 4 drops vanilla extract

TIP:
The sauce can served immediately, but, once it's chilled, it keeps well in the refrigerator. Reheat gently in a double boiler.

1	Put the sugar and water in a saucepan. Heat gently.	2	Allow the sugar to dissolve, tilting the saucepan slightly.	3	Let the caramel cook. Once it's a golden honey color, remove from the heat.
4	Add the butter and whiskey, and mix with a spatula.	5	Add the cream and stir to mix. If there are lumps, return to a low heat and stir.	6	Remove from the heat and add the salt and vanilla. Enjoy with crepes (see recipe idea 79*).

ICE CREAM WITH NOUGAT FOAM

YIELD: 4 SERVINGS • INCLUDES 1 BATCH OF NOUGAT FOAM

Nougat foam goes well with chestnut ice cream. Accompany with a little whipped cream (see recipe 78), if desired.

NOTE: The combination of nougat and chestnut and is very festive. Nougat foam also works well with apple crepes or even on panna cotta.

CREPES WITH CARAMEL AND WHIPPED CREAM

YIELD: 4 SERVINGS • INCLUDES 1 BATCH OF WHIPPED CREAM & 1 BATCH OF CARAMEL SAUCE

❖ 1. Brown 2 to 3 apples cut into segments in 1 knob butter. Add a little cinnamon and mash with a fork.
❖ 2. Heat 4 homemade or store-bought wheat crepes in butter.
❖ 3. Garnish with the apples, hot caramel sauce and whipped cream.

CRÈME ANGLAISE

YIELD: 2 CUPS (500 ML) • PREPARATION: 15 MINUTES • COOKING: 20 MINUTES • RESTING: 15 MINUTES

1 vanilla bean
2⅓ cups (575 ml) whole milk
6 egg yolks
4 to 5 tablespoons (60 to 75 ml) sugar

PRELIMINARY:
Slice the vanilla bean in half lengthwise.

VARIATION:
You can substitute a few cardamom pods for the vanilla. Discard the cardamom after the infusion.

1 2

3 4

1	Heat the milk with the vanilla bean in a saucepan. Once the milk begins to boil, remove from the heat and allow the vanilla to infuse for 15 minutes.	2	In a large saucepan, whisk the egg yolks with the sugar, without creating a lot of foam.
3	Strain the milk into the egg yolk mixture and whisk to incorporate. Scrape the seeds from the vanilla bean and add to the mixture.	4	Cook over very low heat, stirring constantly, until the sauce adheres to the spoon. If the cream “separates,” remove from the heat, whisk vigorously to smooth out and then return to the heat.

BUTTERSCOTCH SAUCE

YIELD: 4 SERVINGS • PREPARATION: 10 MINUTES • COOKING: 10 MINUTES

½ cup (125 ml) brown sugar
3 tablespoons (45 ml) butter (unsalted or salted)
5 tablespoons (75 ml) agave nectar or golden syrup
1 tablespoon (15 ml) cognac
⅔ cup (150 ml) light cream (20%)
1 pinch salt

VARIATION:

You can prepare a non-alcoholic sauce and flavor it with a few drops of vanilla extract.

Agave nectar can be found in large supermarkets, health food stores and specialty stores. Golden syrup can be found in large supermarkets and specialty food stores. You can replace either with a mild-tasting liquid honey or corn syrup.

1	Gently melt together the sugar, butter, nectar or syrup and cognac.	2	Stir until the sugar dissolves. Continue cooking a few minutes, without stirring.
3	Remove from the heat and gradually add the cream (watch out for splatters).	4	Stir (still off the heat) for 2 to 3 minutes, until you obtain a smooth sauce. Add the salt. Once it has cooled, the sauce keeps well in the refrigerator. Reheat gently in a double boiler.

APPLE PIE

YIELD: 4 SERVINGS • INCLUDES 1 BATCH OF CRÈME ANGLAISE AND/OR CARAMEL SAUCE

1. Line a pie pan with shortcrust pastry and refrigerate.
2. Slice 8 apples into wedges. Lightly fry, stirring constantly, in 3 tablespoons (45 ml) butter until golden. Add 1 tablespoon (15 ml) brown sugar. Fill the chilled piecrust.
3. Whip 1 egg, 7 tablespoons (105 ml) crème fraîche or sour cream and 1 tablespoon (15 ml) sugar. Pour over the apples.
4. Bake for 30 minutes at 350°F (180°C). Serve with crème anglaise and/or caramel sauce.

ICE CREAM WITH BUTTERSCOTCH SAUCE

YIELD: 4 SERVINGS • INCLUDES 1 BATCH OF BUTTERSCOTCH SAUCE

Serve the sauce over 2 cups (500 ml) ice cream or frozen yogurt with a few meringue shards — but not too many because the sauce and ice cream are already sweet — and 1 spoonful yogurt. You can also add 1 dash limoncello.

STRAWBERRY COULIS

YIELD: ABOUT 1¼ CUPS (310 ML) • PREPARATION: 15 MINUTES

1 pound (500 g) strawberries
2 tablespoons (30 ml) sugar, or more or less, to taste
1 lemon, juiced
Pepper, to taste (optional)

VARIATION:
You can spice up this coulis with 1 or 2 teaspoons (5 to 10 ml) balsamic vinegar (in which case you'll need to add an extra spoonful or two of sugar). This sauce goes well with vanilla ice cream.

1 2

3 4

1	Rinse and hull the strawberries (remove the stems). Slice in half.	2	Place the strawberries in a food processor.
3	Blend with the sugar and a few drops of lemon juice. Add 1 pinch freshly ground pepper, if desired.	4	Taste and adjust the amount of sugar and lemon as needed.

MANGO COULIS

YIELD: ABOUT 1 CUP (250 ML) • PREPARATION: 10 MINUTES

1. Peel 1 very ripe mango. Remove the pit.

2. Blend with a little lime juice in a food processor.

TIP: You may not need to add sugar because the mango is sometimes very sweet. Taste first and then adjust as needed.

RHUBARB COULIS

YIELD: ABOUT 1¼ CUPS (310 ML) • PREPARATION: 5 MINUTES • COOKING: 30 TO 35 MINUTES

1. Coarsely chop 1 pound (500 g) rhubarb (fresh or frozen) and put in a baking dish along with 2 to 3 tablespoons (30 to 45 ml) sugar and 1 pinch freshly grated ginger (optional). Bake in a 375°F (190°C) oven for 30 to 35 minutes.

2. Blend in a food processor. If needed, strain and thin with a little water. Taste and add sugar if needed.

CHOCOLATE SAUCE

YIELD: ABOUT 1 CUP (250 ML) • PREPARATION: 15 MINUTES • COOKING: 5 MINUTES

7 ounces (100 g) dark chocolate
½ cup (125 ml) light cream (20%)
2 teaspoons (10 ml) unsalted butter

VARIATIONS:
This sauce can be flavored as desired by first infusing 1 vanilla bean, 2 to 3 cardamom pods, a cinnamon stick or Earl Grey tea in the milk. You can even add 1 tablespoon (15 ml) rum or cognac at the end. You can also use salted butter, if desired.

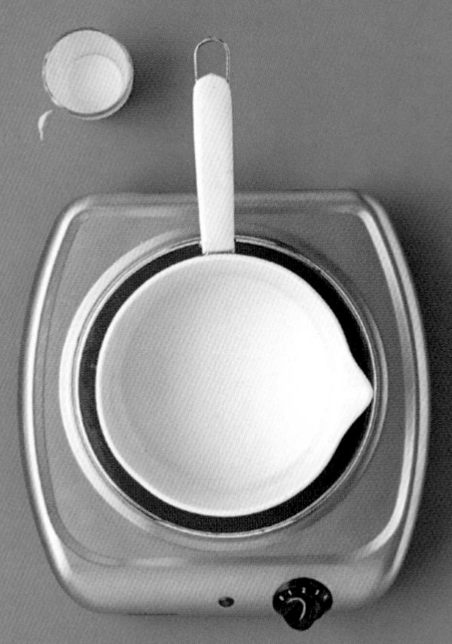

1 2

3 4

1	Chop the chocolate.	2	Heat the cream.
3	Once the cream begins to boil, remove it from the heat and add the chocolate and butter.	4	Whisk. It's ready! The sauce keeps well in the refrigerator. To use, simply reheat very gently and whisk, if needed. **SERVING SUGGESTION:** Pear pie tart (see recipe idea 85*).

82*, 83*, 84*

PANNA COTTA

YIELD: 4 SERVINGS • INCLUDES 1 BATCH OF STRAWBERRY, MANGO OR RHUBARB COULIS

⊹ 1. Soften 4 teaspoons (20 ml) unflavored gelatin powder in water.

⊹ 2. Heat 2½ cups (625 ml) heavy cream (36%) with 1 vanilla bean sliced in half, the finely grated zest of 1 lemon and 6 tablespoons (90 ml) sugar. Stir. Once the cream begins to boil, remove from the heat and dissolve the gelatin in it.

⊹ 3. Pour into molds and let cool in the refrigerator for a few hours. Serve with the coulis of your choice.

PEAR TART

YIELD: 6 SERVINGS • INCLUDES 1 BATCH OF CHOCOLATE SAUCE

⇠ 1. Line a pie pan with shortcrust pastry and refrigerate.
⇠ 2. Slice 6 ripe or cooked pears. Sprinkle lemon juice on the cut pears.
⇠ 3. Fill the piecrust.
⇠ 4. Whisk together 1 egg, 7 tablespoons (105 ml) crème fraîche or sour cream and 5 tablespoons (75 ml) sugar. Pour this mixture over the pears.
⇠ 5. Bake for 30 minutes. Serve with chocolate sauce.

ZABAGLIONE

YIELD: 4 SERVINGS • PREPARATION: 20 MINUTES • COOKING: 10 MINUTES

4 egg yolks
3 to 4 tablespoons (45 to 60 ml) sugar
½ cup (125 ml) fruity white wine

STORAGE:
You can store zabaglione in the refrigerator for a few hours. Take it out ahead of time so that it can warm to room temperature before using, otherwise it will fall apart.

VARIATION:
You can replace the white wine with muscat, champagne or lemon juice (in which case you'll need to add sugar).

1 2

3 4

1	Whisk together the egg yolks and sugar in a heatproof bowl, until the mixture pales and foams.	2	Gradually add the wine, whisking constantly.
3	Put the bowl over a pot of simmering water to make a double boiler. Whisk constantly until the mixture foams and increases in volume, about 5 to 10 minutes.	4	Serve immediately. If you don't want to serve the zabaglione right away, continue whisking it off the heat until it cools.

LEMON CURD

YIELD: 3 CUPS (750 ML) • PREPARATION: 15 MINUTES • COOKING: 20 MINUTES

4 lemons
4 eggs
2 cups (500 ml) sugar
7 tablespoons (105 ml) butter, cut into pieces

VARIATION:
Use limes or replace 1 lemon with 1 orange.

1 2

3 4

1	Zest and juice the lemons. Whisk the eggs in a bowl.	2	Place the lemon zest and juice, sugar and butter in a double boiler. Cook, stirring, until the sugar dissolves.
3	Add the eggs and gently cook (do not boil), stirring constantly.	4	It's ready once the mixture adheres to the spoon. You can pair lemon curd with short-bread cookies to make express lemon tartlets (see recipe idea 87*).

ICE CREAM WITH BERRIES AND ZABAGLIONE

YIELD: 4 SERVINGS • INCLUDES 1 BATCH OF ZABAGLIONE

Serve the zabaglione on berry ice cream garnished with a few fresh berries. You can also use frozen berries (allow 14 ounces/400 g for 4 servings).

Thaw the berries by placing them in a saucepan with 1 or 2 tablespoons (15 to 30 ml) confectioners' sugar, according to taste.

SHORTBREADS WITH LEMON CURD

YIELD: 4 SERVINGS • INCLUDES 1 BATCH OF LEMON CURD

Buy shortbread cookies and spread lemon curd on them to make instant lemon tartlets.

VARIATION:
To make a lemon pie, fill a baked piecrust bottom with the curd, cover with meringue, if desired, and bake in a 350°F (180°C) oven for 10 minutes.

APPENDIXES

INGREDIENTS AND CULINARY TERMS

TABLE OF SAUCES

TABLE OF CONTENTS

RECIPE INDEX

SUBJECT INDEX

ACKNOWLEDGMENTS

INGREDIENTS AND CULINARY TERMS

ANCHOVIES
Anchovies in oil are a powerful seasoning for sauces made to accompany cold meats, among other foods. You can crumble the fillets with a fork or chop them with a knife before incorporating them into the other ingredients.

BREAK
A sauce is said to break when the emulsion on which it's based separates. The fat separates from the other ingredients, and the sauce looks as if it has the fat on one side and the solids or other liquids on the other side. Sometimes you have to throw out the sauce, but sometimes you can save it. If a mayonnaise breaks, you can restart the emulsion by using another egg yolk (which contains an emulsifying agent) and gradually adding the broken sauce and remaining oil to that yolk.

BROWN SAUCES
This is one of the large families of sauces. They are made from brown stocks, brown roux, different liquids and various aromatic ingredients (including wine, other alcohols, onion or bacon), which are added, one at time, to the sauce's base and cooked or reduced to enhance their flavor. These ingredients form, in the final sauce, a layering of flavors that are particularly remarkable. Brown sauces take a long time to prepare. One example of a brown sauce in this book is a relatively simple and quick version of marchand de vin sauce (literally "wine merchant" sauce). The "mother sauces" of the brown sauce family are espagnole sauce (which includes an aromatic blend of carrots, celery, onions, beef stock and tomato) and demi-glace (an espagnole sauce with mushrooms and Madeira).

CHUTNEY
Originally an Indian mixture, this condiment is based on vegetables, herbs and packaged seasonings. In the case of this book, they are fresh sauces that combine lively ingredients that are spicy or soothing, including mint, cilantro, coconut and spices.

COURT-BOUILLON
A stock made from vegetables and herbs and sometimes wine, lemon juice or vinegar. It is traditionally used to poach fish, seafood or vegetables.

CRÈME ANGLAISE
French for "English cream," a crème anglaise is a rich custard sauce. It can be poured over cakes, fruit and other desserts and can be flavored in any number of ways.

CRÈME FRAÎCHE
Popular in France and throughout Europe, crème fraîche (literally "fresh cream") is a thick, tangy cream with a texture similar to sour cream, which is a good substitute for it. You can make your own crème fraîche by mixing 1 cup (250 ml) whipping cream and 2 tablespoons (30 ml) buttermilk or sour cream in a glass container. Cover and let stand at room temperature (60°F to 85°F/15°C to 30°C) for 8 to 24 hours, until very thick. Stir well, cover and refrigerate for at least 4 hours and up to 10 days.

FOAM
An essential preparation of molecular cooking, it's a light mousse made with a siphon (a pressurized canister that can tolerate hot ingredients). The siphon injects a dose of nitrous oxide into a very fluid mixture, creating a fleeting foamy texture.

GREEK-STYLE YOGURT
Also called strained yogurt, yogurt cheese and simply Greek yogurt, it is plain yogurt that has been strained to remove the whey (the liquid), creating a thick, spreadable product. You can make your own by lining a strainer with cheesecloth, filling with plain yogurt and leaving to drain for a few hours or overnight.

MOTHER SAUCE
This is the basic recipe for a large family of sauces, which is used to make all the various sauces in that family. Béchamel is the mother sauce of the béchamel family (which includes soubise and

Mornay), whereas hollandaise is the mother sauce of the sauces based on melted butter and an egg emulsion that must be kept hot (like béarnaise). Velouté is also a mother sauce that produces multiple variations (such as Bercy and supreme). Espagnole sauce is the mother sauce of brown sauces (such as bordelaise and marchand de vin).

RAITA

Originally an Indian mixture, raitas are generally based on yogurt, raw vegetables, fruit (such as bananas), mild herbs and spices. They soothe the palate when eating a very spicy dish. A raita can also be used as a refreshing accompaniment to any simmered dish or chicken dish (such as fried chicken, leftover roast chicken or chicken skewers).

REDUCE

Reduce the volume of a liquid mixture by boiling or simmering. The reduction is the end result. The process helps to concentrate flavors. For example, a vinegar reduction with shallot and tarragon is the aromatic base of béarnaise (you can even throw away the herbs and the shallot, as all of their flavor is in the reduction).

RELISH

This name is given to modest yet tasty little mixtures that delight the palate, as the name suggests. Relishes are often made with garlic, to bring out the flavor of simple dishes.

ROUGAIL

A highly spiced condiment that is popular in the West Indies and Réunion. It often accompanies vegetable dishes, shellfish, fish and rice dishes.

ROUX

A roux is a melted butter and flour mixture that is added to thicken a sauce, of which it is the base. The mixture is made in a saucepan and is cooked, stirring, for varying lengths of time. If cooked for less than 5 minutes it's a white roux (for a béchamel, for example). If cooked for 6 to 7 minutes it's a blond roux, with a more noticeable color and a slight hazelnut taste (such as for a velouté). Anything cooked for longer than 8 to 9 minutes is a brown roux.

SALSA

Originally South American, salsa means "sauce" in Spanish. In this book the term is used to describe a sauce made of chopped raw ingredients, such as tomatoes, fruits, herbs, chili peppers and the like. Salsas enhance simmered dishes (such as chili con carne, boeuf bourguignon or soup) and lightly season grilled meats and fish. You can also dip tortilla chips in it, of course!

STRAIN

To filter a mixture through a strainer or chinois (a conical sieve with a very fine mesh) in order to obtain a sauce with a fine texture. The idea is to eliminate any bits or lumps, keeping only the flavor of any solid ingredients in the final mixture, which will be smooth and fluid. Sometimes the strainer needs to be lined with cheesecloth to create an even finer strainer.

VELOUTÉ

This is one of the large families of sauces. A velouté is, more or less, a béchamel in which the milk is replaced by stock. It's flavored with shallots and white wine and prepared using a fish, vegetable or poultry stock. It can be used as is with poultry, white meats and fish, but it can also serve as a base for gratins, pies and lasagna.

WHISK

Use an electric mixer with a whisk attachment or a hand whisk that is fairly long, oval or flat, which will help scrape the bottom of bowls or saucepans. Whisking helps increase the volume of a sauce while preserving the emulsion, such as when making mayonnaise, béarnaise and hollandaise sauces, Caesar dressing and certain vinaigrettes.

ZEST

Citrus zest is a welcome addition to many sauces: it contains essential oils with a strong scent. Ideally it's removed from the fruit using the fine side of a grater or using a special rasp (like a Microplane). Traditional zesters often produce zest that is too big to use in sauces.

TABLE OF SAUCES

	Cooked Meats	Cold Meats	Poultry	White Fish	Fatty Fish	Salads & Raw Vegetables	Cooked Vegetables & Soups	Pasta
Béchamel			+	+			+	
Béarnaise	+							
Hollandaises							+	
Beurre Blanc				+	+		+	
Blue Cheese	+							
Green Peppercorn	+							
Bercy			+	+	+			
Marchand de Vin	+							
Meat Gravy	+		+				+	
Gribiche		+						
Mayonnaise			+			+	+	
Aioli				+			+	
Green Goddess Dressing		+	+					
Tartar Sauce		+			+	+		
Marie Rose	+					+		
Rouille				+			+	
Classic Pesto	+	+			+		+	+
Pistachio Pesto	+						+	+
Watercress Pesto	+				+		+	+
Mint Pesto	+						+	+
Red Pesto							+	+
Classic Tomato		+						+
Arrabiata								+
Puttanesca		+						
Express Bolognese								+
Vodka Sauce								+
Roasted Tomato		+			+			+
Raw Tomato								+
Three-Tomato					+			
Lemon Cream			+	+				
Aglio e Olio								+
Tomato Salsa	+		+	+			+	
Mango-Almond Salsa				+	+			
Tomato-Ginger Rougail	+		+		+			
Chimichurri	+				+			
Guacamole			+		+	+		
Fresh Mint Chutney	+	+			+			

	Cooked Meats	Cold Meats	Poultry	White Fish	Fatty Fish	Salads & Raw Vegetables	Cooked Vegetables & Soups	Pasta
Cilantro-Coconut Chutney			+		+		+	
Creamy Chutney			+			+		
Cucumber Raita			+					
Bell Pepper Relish	+				+			
Anchovy Sauce	+	+						
Chopped Anchovy Sauce	+	+						
Green Sauce	+				+		+	
Green Sauce with Orange					+		+	
Apple Horseradish Sauce	+	+						
Mustard Sauce				+	+			
Vanilla Sauce			+	+	+			
Homemade Ketchup	+		+		+			
Gado Gado			+	+	+	+	+	
Roasted Zucchini	+							
Carrot			+		+			
Fava Bean	+				+			
Roasted Eggplant	+		+	+		+		
Artichoke	+					+		
Ginger Soy			+	+	+		+	
Teriyaki	+				+			
Green Curry			+	+	+		+	
Classic Vinaigrette						+	+	
Lemon Zest Vinaigrette					+	+	+	
Ras el Hanout Vinaigrette			+			+	+	
Hazelnut Vinaigrette						+	+	
Garlic Vinaigrette			+			+	+	
Citrus Vinaigrette					+	+		
Cambodian Vinaigrette			+			+	+	
Japanese Vinaigrette			+			+	+	
Honey-Mustard Vinaigrette		+				+		
Blue Cheese Dressing			+			+		
Caesar Salad Dressing			+			+	+	
Cuban Mojo Dressing			+			+	+	
Mushroom Foam							+	
Foie Gras Foam	+		+				+	
Coconut Foam			+				+	
Ham Foam							+	

TABLE OF CONTENTS

1

THE CLASSICS

2

PASTA SAUCES

3

CONTEMPORARY SAUCES

4

SALAD DRESSINGS

5

FOAMS

6

SWEET SAUCES

RECIPE INDEX

INDEX OF RECIPE IDEAS

SUBJECT INDEX

ACKNOWLEDGMENTS

Thank you to Sonia, Fred, Nina, Ange and Mona (family ambience), Julia (ideas and advice), Audrey (endurance) and Rosemarie (impetus).

BHV DÉCO
www.bhv.fr

HABITAT
www.habitat.net

IKEA
www.ikea.com

LE BON MARCHÉ
www.lebonmarché.fr

MONOPRIX
www.monoprix.fr

MUJI
www.muji.fr

THE CONRAN SHOP
www.conran.com